The Field Worker in
IMMIGRANT HEALTH

Edited by

J. S. DODGE

Senior Medical Officer (Epidemiology),
City of Bradford

STAPLES PRESS

FIRST PUBLISHED 1969 BY STAPLES PRESS
3 UPPER JAMES STREET GOLDEN SQUARE LONDON WI
COPYRIGHT © STAPLES PRESS 1969
PRINTED IN GREAT BRITAIN BY
EBENEZER BAYLIS AND SON LIMITED
THE TRINITY PRESS
WORCESTER AND LONDON

SBN 286 62716 7

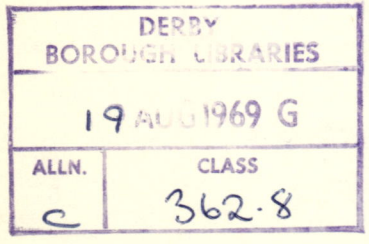

CONTRIBUTORS

F. N. Bamford, M.D., D.P.H., D.C.H., Principal Medical Officer (Child Health), City of Bradford.

H. P. Burrowes, M.B., B.S., D.P.H., D.P.M., Principal Medical Officer (Mental Health and Child Guidance), City of Bradford.

J. S. Dodge, M.B., B.S., L.R.C.P., M.R.C.S., D.T.M. & H., D.P.H., Senior Medical Officer (Epidemiology), City of Bradford.

K. M. Lumb, M.B., CH.B., D.(OBST.), R.C.O.G., D.C.H., D.P.H., Senior Medical Officer (Maternity and Child Welfare), City of Bradford.

F. H. Myers, M.R.S.H., M.A.P.H.I., Chief Public Health Inspector, City of Bradford.

The author or authors of each chapter are shown in the list of contents.

CONTENTS

Preface   *Page* 11

1 **Whys and Wherefores:** *J. S. Dodge*   13

Reasons for population movement; deficiencies in the
social services; attitudes towards strangers.

2 **Population Movement:** *J. S. Dodge*   17

The epidemiology of population movement; transmission
of disease; formation of a susceptible population; alteration in patterns of health and disease.

3 **Culture and Custom:** *J. S. Dodge and K. M. Lumb*   28

Religion; religious prohibition of certain foods; diet;
purdah; marriage and divorce; names and naming;
hygiene and sanitation; disposal of the dead.

4 **Immigrants and the Law:** *J. S. Dodge*   45

Aliens; the background to the Commonwealth Immigration Acts; the Acts described; the Race Relations Act.

5 **The Immigrant and the Public Health Law:** *J. S.*
Dodge and F. H. Myers   57

Housing; overcrowding and multiple occupation;
rented houses; house purchase; rental purchase; slum
clearance; Food Hygiene Regulations; Food and Drugs
Act; meat; slaughter houses; the Shops Act.

6 **The Migrant and Mental Health:** *H. P. Burrowes*   71

Change of home; stress; stress on adults and stress on
children; the appearance of mental disease; stress
disorders.

7   **Childbirth, Child Feeding and Family Planning:**   77
J. S. Dodge and K. M. Lumb

Ante-natal clinics; ante-natal care; communication difficulties; fasting; the delivery; infant feeding; weaning; gastro-enteritis; vitamin supplements; family planning; communication.

8   **The Nutrition of Immigrant Children:** *F. N.*   89
Bamford

Basic nutrition; infant feeding; heights and weights; anaemia; vitamin deficiencies; fasting.

9   **Children separated from their Families:** *F. N.*
Bamford   94

Fostering; Children's Act 1958; child minding; Public Health Act 1968; stimulation of intellectual development; division of families.

10   **The Immigrant Child at School:** *J. S. Dodge*   99

Settling in; medical examination; non-English speaking children; differences of dress; fasting and feeding; school–parent contact; child care by relatives; stress of adaptation; parental attitudes.

11   **The Immigrant and Infectious Diseases:** *J. S. Dodge*   107

Importation of infectious disease; notification of infectious disease; quarantinable disease; food poisoning.

12   **Quarantinable Diseases:** *J. S. Dodge*   113

The quarantinable diseases; International Sanitary Regulations; International Certificates of Immunization and Vaccination; surveillance.

13   **Other Imported Diseases:** *J. S. Dodge*   122

Differential loading on the health services; fevers;

typhoid and paratyphoid; poliomyelitis; yaws; trachoma; diphtheria; cholera; leprosy; malaria.

14 **Tuberculosis Control:** *J. S. Dodge* 130

Epidemiology of tuberculosis; eradication of tuberculosis; control of tuberculosis in an immigrant population; case finding and contact tracing.

15 **Venereal Disease:** *J. S. Dodge* 142

The basic epidemiology of the disease; the unattached male; the law concerning V.D.; methods of control; contact tracing.

16 **Helminthic Infestation:** *F. H. Bamford* 153

Frequency of infection; threadworm; dwarf tapeworm; roundworm; whipworm; hookworm; beef and pork tapeworm; filariasis; schistosomiasis; transmission and the public health.

APPENDICES

I **Action** to be taken by the Health Department following the arrival of an immigrant and his family: *J. S. Dodge* 163

II **Immunization and Vaccination:** *J. S. Dodge* 165

Protection of the child; smallpox vaccination in relation to other immunizations.

III **Vital Statistics:** *J. S. Dodge* 168

The need for vital statistics; the necessity for certain basic facts to be known before statistics are uttered.

IV **Housing Standards of Fitness:** *J. S. Dodge* 171

Housing standards of fitness; unfit houses; action on unfit houses; closing orders; unfitness orders; clearance areas; development areas; Rent Act 1957.

V 1967: Migrant Workers in Western Europe   174

Glossary   176

Book List   180

Index   183

PREFACE

THE OBJECT of this book is to provide information and ideas for the field worker in an immigrant community. The intention is to state the basic principles involved and to give enough details to illustrate and explain them. Further details should be obtained by wider reading, by conversation with immigrants and by experience: the first of these is catered for in this book by a book list and it is hoped that the book itself will make the second more easy and the third less painful.

The term *immigrant* has been so misused that it has ceased to be a reliable means of identifying a person. In this book the term *immigrant* means one who has come into a new community and who is adjusting to that community, such adjustment being both biological and psychological. The use of the term *immigrant* solely to mean a person of African or Asian descent, is to be deprecated on grounds of inaccuracy alone.

The term *field worker* is intended to embrace health visitors, midwives, health inspectors, social workers, district nurses, school nurses and all those whose work brings them in contact with men, women and children who are adapting to a new environment. Although the book is primarily for the health worker, it is hoped that it will be of help to those in a wider sphere of interests and concerned with people in their homes, school and work place.

The term 'health' is used in the sense of the Anglo-Saxon *haelth* from which it is derived, meaning a state of wholeness: it includes mental health as much as bodily health. The interaction of mind and body in health and illhealth occurs in the immigrant population to the same extent as in the indigenous one. However, evaluation of the various factors involved is more difficult where there is a marked difference in the cultural background between the immigrant and the field worker. This difficulty is exacerbated by a language barrier but the differences in custom and culture are more important. There is much more to communication than hiring an interpreter.

Health must not be considered to be merely the absence of illhealth: it is a positive state of physical and mental wellbeing in a person in an environment to which he can adapt without over-straining his powers of adaptation.

It is not the intention of this book to provide solutions for all problems and it is doubtful whether this is, in any case, possible. All human beings have their similarities and their differences: their response to disease and stress will follow basic patterns but there will be individual differences which may be so marked as to obscure the basic cause. Observation of these differences will be more difficult if the observer has a different culture and the means of communication between patient and field worker is less than adequate. It is hoped that this book will make the similarities easier to appreciate.

Any writing on health tends to concentrate on illhealth: the immigrant should not be expected to display every condition described herein any more than the people in the doctor's surgery display all the conditions described in the latest medical textbook.

CHAPTER I

WHYS AND WHEREFORES

THERE ARE two main reasons why migration of population groups occurs. The first is escape from religious, political or ethnic persecution and the second the obtaining of work. The second reason implies that there is a shortage of work in the 'donor' country and available work in the receptor country, and where large numbers are involved there is likely to be either general or regional under-employment. Encouragement of immigration by the host country also implies the need to increase the labour force.

Immigration from Ireland towards the latter stages of the industrial revolution in the middle of the nineteenth century was consequent on shortage of work in Ireland and the need for large armies of labourers for constructional work, particularly railway building. Immigration from Poland at the beginning of the second world war and from Hungary in 1960 stemmed from political persecution. Immigration of Jews in the latter part of the 1930s followed ethnic persecution and the immigration of the Huguenots in the sixteenth century followed religious persecution. Immigration from Commonwealth countries since the end of the second world war has been mainly due to the search for work and to recruitment for work on the part of the host government: the movement has sometimes been affected by political events, for example, the immigration of Cypriots and the influx of Kenya Asians, but the main feature has remained the search for work.

Work is generally more available in areas of expansion than in areas of static or diminishing economic growth. In expansion areas the social services always lag behind the growth of population, a growth which is seldom foreseen and usually underestimated: when the growth of population is stimulated by the arrival of work-seeking migrants from outside the country in addition to the shift of the working population within the country, then the burden on the local social services is considerably increased. In general the social services (that is, housing, education, medical, welfare etc.) are provided by local government whereas the ebb and flow of industrial prosperity is dependent on a number of factors most of which are national or supranational and few of which are local in origin: local authorities, even in an area whose prosperity is increasing, do not have the funds or the staff to meet a rapid expansion of their social services and cannot take an adequate share of the increased industrial prosperity, especially in the early days of the expanding population and this is the time when such increased funds have been most needed. The central government has often given assistance but this has generally been too little and too late.

The areas where deficiencies in the social services have been most grave are in housing, education and health. These deficiencies are partly due to increases in the population and partly due to a raising of standards of what is considered to constitute proper care in these fields. For example, there has been a general increase in the overall standard of ante-natal care since the end of the last war and an increase in the proportion of hospital deliveries: it is now considered—and rightly so—by most women in the general population of this country that a hospital delivery is best and concern is expressed if this expectation is not met. Similarly there has been a considerable improvement in teaching standards in this country in the last twenty-five years and parents will be dissatisfied if their expectations are not fulfilled.

It is a regrettable but intensely human trait that when something is amiss, energy tends to be devoted not only to *what* is wrong but also to *who* is wrong. This latter quest is often non-productive as the dereliction of duty or moral error that is implied may very likely be absent. The search for human error as the aetiology of unwelcome shortages may rapidly develop into the blame being laid upon a group of people who may be the unwitting cause or completely innocent in this respect: it is very rare for them to be the conscious and purposeful cause. The characteristic of a group of this nature is that it should be a minority group which is recognizable as a group and has differences from the general population which can render it easily identifiable. The 'young people of today' and the 'old fogies' are minor and almost laughable examples of this: 'Teddyboys', 'Mods and Rockers', 'Jews', 'Germans', 'Communists' and 'Immigrants' are all examples of groups which have incurred displeasure because they are different, and not all of these examples are overwhelmingly humourous.

The 'folk devil' myth is the description given by behavioural psychologists to the establishment of a group as a scapegoat for the fears and worries of the general population.

Many poets and philosophers and a multitude of people who would not so describe themselves have observed that folk have their differences, but in many ways are much the same. This book will examine some of the differences in detail but there will, however, be a generally unwritten assumption that the similarities are equally important; this book deals with human beings, not cyber-men or daleks.

Before one is able adequately to serve the needs of a community, it is necessary to understand the more important differences of belief and custom which distinguish that community. This precept is as relevant for the health visitor from a northern industrial town who goes to work in an East Anglian village as it is for the schoolmaster faced with a class of Asian lads newly arrived from India and Pakistan. This is not to say, of course, that the nature of the differences will be the same.

One is accustomed to speak of barriers to communication and provided the term is not over-used it is a valid description. These barriers may be based on differences of language or culture. If one is unable to communicate with another because of a lack of a common language then one can do little except smile and, although this is pleasant, it is less than adequate for those who have a need to communicate with each other. This barrier can be overcome by the use of an interpreter and then the next barrier is reached—that of culture. If the conversation is confined to 'do you have a cough, stand over there, etc.' then differences of culture are not often apparent: when one begins to communicate as separate person-alities on more complicated matters, then differences of belief and culture are of importance. It is easy for the Western European to observe that the culture of the immigrant is different from his own and as easy to forget that his culture is different from that of the immigrant. It is also easy to offend unwittingly against another person's acceptance of what is right and proper. It is fortunate that most people in all cultural groups do not easily take offence.

Class has become something of an outmoded concept in this country and as portrayed by top hat and cloth cap, port and pheasant and trouble at the mill, is a subject for humour. One does not have to see all human activity in Marxist terms to realize that class barriers exist although they are a little more subtle than in the examples in the last sentence. In some societies class is still important and it is advisable to understand that this is so.

Race is usually given pride of place in an examination of people from different continents, but this does not indicate its true position. It is much less important than differences in language and culture and some would put it as less important than class. It is unfortunate that 'race' has become an emotive word and in some quarters a term of abuse, especially when it is not mentioned as such. There is little acceptance of the belief that because a person is of a particular race, then *ipso facto*, he or she is inferior (or, in the other direction, superior); some rather warped minds see the matter in these terms: such people are in a very small minority and when their ideas are expressed in this form, they find little general favour. The more popular mode of expression is that because a person is of a different race, he is *ipso facto* different—which is undeniably true but this is not to imply that the difference is for the worse or that members of the same race, or nationality, exhibit the same differences. It is significant that a number of basic prejudices about racial differences are less commonly seen in those who have met and communicated with people of the race in question.

CHAPTER 2

POPULATION MOVEMENT

BASICALLY, population movement is of two sorts: firstly, a natural movement, and secondly, a journeying movement of population from one place to another.

Natural movement is concerned with birth, death, marriage and is expressed in the familiar 'vital statistics' where these happenings are expressed either as a whole number or as a rate per hundred or thousand of the total or comparative populations: for example, the number of births per thousand population or so many deaths per thousand population. The basic data of the matter may well be summarized as 'hatches, matches and dispatches.' These rates form the index of effectiveness of preventive and curative health measures, and, providing that care is always taken to make sure that what is being compared one with another is in fact comparable, are of inestimable value both in planning for the maintenance of health and combatting of disease, and in replanning and assessing the progress of measures of curative and preventive medicine.

The second type of movement is the actual journeying movement of a population from one place to another, and is the type usually associated with the term 'population movement' by those other than vital statisticians. The term 'population' is used to indicate a group of people. They are usually a part or section of a larger group of people and will exhibit similarities one part with another as well as differences. The term 'population movement' may be used in a way that implies the movement of a single person as opposed to a number of people.

Natural movement will not be further considered here.

Movement of groups of the population, sometimes in small numbers, sometimes amounting to a total migration of a complete population, is recorded throughout the history of man and was a feature of prehistoric times. Population movement is today extremely common and occurs in a number of ways; the drift, particularly of young men from rural societies into the towns where they hope to make their fortunes is as common today as ever it was: the movement of individuals or of family groups from one place to another to seek work or change of workplace is also common and this type of movement may often be a seasonal one. For example, a number of workers come to this country from continental Europe to supplement the local labour force in the catering industry in the holiday towns and this seasonal migration for work occurs in many countries. In some areas of the world there are groups of people who are wholly migrant and spend their lives moving from one place to another in association with herds of cattle, sheep and other animals. Such nomads are no longer a feature of life in this country apart perhaps from the gipsies, and these, by and large, no longer rely on trade in animals for their livelihood. At the present time more and more journeys are undertaken for trading reasons and representatives and salesmen of trading organizations spend much of their time travelling, often from one country to another. Also in this country, in common with many others, the desire to travel away to other countries or to other parts of the same country for holidays is an increasingly common part of everyday life. All this involves journeying movement of a population from one place to another: the term 'population' is generally applied to a group of people but the same basic problem is met with when a single individual moves.

The term 'immigrant' is usually used to describe a person who has moved from one place to another and intends to remain and reside at the place of his final destination for a reasonable period; the duration of the intended residence taken by the Registrar General in compilation of his statistics with regard to immigrants is one year and this, therefore, rules out holiday makers, the business man and the short term student, although these three groups may be associated with importation of diseases from the country of origin to the receptor country. The traveller who is passing through a country is less liable to acquire a disease than a resident of that country, although bowel infections are sometimes an exception to this general rule. The basic public health problems are similar with regard to all travellers but will vary in detail according to the type of traveller.

The journeying type of population movement, hereinafter referred to as population movement, may be of three basic types. These are shown diagrammatically in Figure 1.

Firstly, movement may occur from country A to country B (example X). Secondly, movement may occur from country A to

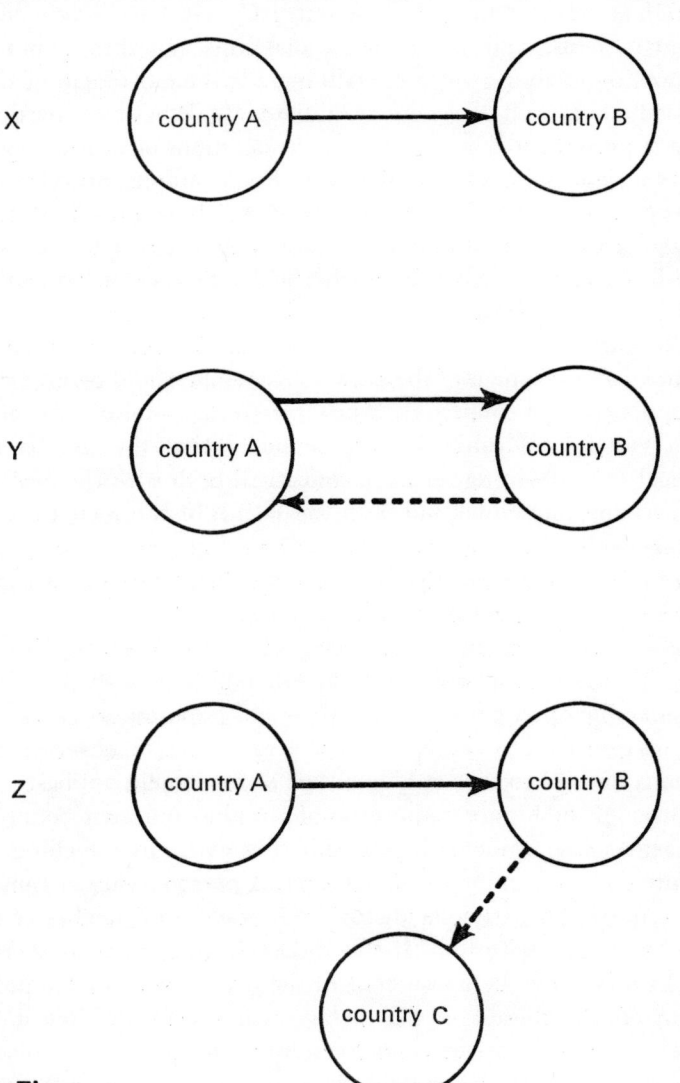

Fig. 1

country B and also from B to country A: those travelling from country B to country A may include some of those who had previously travelled from country A to country B (example Y). Thirdly, population movement may occur from country A to country B and from country B to country C: again, some persons travelling from country B to country C may have originated in country A (example Z). In these diagrams and throughout this section, population movement will include the movement of single individuals as well as groups of individuals. Whether a particular type of movement is important in considerations of health depends on the view point of the observer. For example, movement of persons from country A to country B will have no effect on the incidence of imported disease in country A, whereas to the public health service in country B this particular type of movement will be of prime importance.

The three basic examples in figure 1 are labelled X, Y and Z. Figure 2 shows which of the basic movements would be important to an observer in country A, B or C, from the point of view of the preservation of Health. It will be noted that the middle four vertical columns in figure 2 are concerned both with the health of the arriving individual and with the health of the receptor community while the column on the extreme right of figure 2 refers only to the personal health of the individual and with the intending traveller rather than the arriving traveller.

Life is seldom as simple as a diagram and in practice, all three types of movement will occur together although there will be considerable differences in magnitude and importance—these two not necessarily coinciding. It is a very fortunate observer who stations himself so that only one type of movement applies.

Although in Figure 1 the example implies different countries, the same basic epidemiological situation exists in travelling, for example, from London to Manchester. A person living in London and acquiring a particular disease may travel to Manchester and take his disease with him. If this disease is transmissable then he will be a factor to be considered in the preservation of the public health of Manchester. If his disease is non-transmissable it will merely be a factor in the consideration of the treatment of disease

Manchester. At the present time, travelling between London

	imported diseases from Country A	imported diseases from Country B	acquired diseases in Country B	acquired diseases in Country C	personal protection of the intending traveller
observer in Country A		Y			X Y Z
observer in Country B·	X Y Z		X Y Z		Y Z
observer in Country C	Z	Z	Z	Z	

Important factors in consideration of the preservation of health

}

X—movement as in example X

Y—movement as in example Y

Z—movement as in example Z

Fig. 2

and Manchester is so common and so frequently indulged in by so many people that, except for a few highly infectious and important diseases, the arrival of a person in Manchester from London would be un-noted by the health authorities of that city. However, at the time of the great plague in the seventeenth century, the arrival of a person from London might be extremely significant in the consideration of the health of the receptor city.

Because the disease patterns of Manchester and London are generally equivalent, population movement from one is unlikely to be a significant influence on the health of the other. Because the disease patterns are similar, the general immune state and resistance to infectious disease is also likely to be similar. Another consideration is that the populations of the two cities are of the same racial group and, therefore, any racial differences in the susceptibility to disease will be unimportant. If one considers the case of a man arriving in London from Delhi, the position may be different. Firstly, the disease patterns of Delhi and London may be significantly different, both from the point of view of endemic disease and from the point of view of epidemic disease. The traveller, therefore, is more likely to be importing an unaccustomed disease into the receptor city than would be the case if two cities had a similar basic disease endemicity. Because of the different disease background the traveller may be more liable to infection with a particular disease prevalent in the receptor city than would the normal population of the receptor area, and this difference may be further modified by a difference in racial susceptibility to disease. Differences in climate and food generally play a small part unless the traveller is unaware of the particular hazards of his new climate. He may, from ignorance or from non-availability of accustomed food take less food than is necessary in the receptor country and this may influence the natural history of his diseases, both imported and newly acquired.

Influence of Genetically Transmissable Diseases

A number of diseases which are dependant for their spread on genetic transmission from parent to offspring are more frequently seen in tropical and subtropical countries than in this country. Although these diseases are not common and not of great public health importance when considered alongside the main endemic and epidemic diseases, yet their existence in consideration of the health of the individual (as opposed to the public health) should be noted.

An important group of these diseases is characterised by the possession of a haemoglobin molecule which is abnormal and anaemia is a common presenting symptom. Investigation of anaemia in an immigrant should therefore include tests to diagnose any of these conditions and if their presence is established this may involve genetic counselling to parents and to the children affected. It must be stressed that these diseases are not common.

Changes in the Reservoir of Infection

The arrival of a significant number of immigrants may influence the health of the indigenous population by an increase in the size of the reservoir of infection of endemic disease. An example of this is tuberculosis. If the overall incidence of tuberculosis in the total population is increased by the arrival of an immigrant group then because the infective pool of the disease is larger, the potential for the disease to spread is greater. Spread may occur within the immigrant population or between the immigrant population and indigenous one: the amount of infection passing from one community to another will depend on the degree of interaction between the two communities. By and large, this is not very great in the early days of the arrival of an immigrant group. Spread of a disease may also occur within the indigenous community. Of course, spread of infection between communities may equally well take place in the opposite direction. An increase in the reservoir of infection may arise in two ways; either the disease may be imported through the advent of a population with a higher overall morbidity rate from the disease or by the importation of a more susceptible population who acquire the disease more readily than the indigenous population and exhibit a higher morbidity from the disease which they have caught after their arrival. Both these factors are operative in the epidemiology of tuberculosis in areas which have recently received significant numbers of immigrants from the Asian or African continents.

Influence of the New Environment

The disease pattern in the immigrant population may be further modified by the unfamiliar environment in which the new community finds itself. If housing is in short supply, then overcrowding will be common. If the menfolk precede their families then the overcrowding will be seen in the establishment of houses of multiple occupation and consisting of a number of men living together, sharing the rent, the housekeeping expenses and the household chores, including the cooking. Such a change may assist the spread of an infectious disease in the immigrant community; this will increase the general reservoir of infection either within the immigrant community or in the general population and thus increase the rate of spread of the infection. At that stage not only is the infection increasing by an increase of the numbers involved but the rate of increase is also rising. This would be confined largely to the immigrant community at first, but it would in time spread outside that community, the rate at which it did so depending on the infectiousness of the disease, the route of spread, and the degree of contact between the two communities. At this point the immunological state of the indigenous community would become an important factor. It should be noted that the working environment is of importance both from the viewpoint of environmental health as well as intra-community and inter-community spread of infectious disease.

In the above paragraphs consideration is given to the ways in which the patterns of disease in the immigrants and in the host community may be altered: it does not necessarily follow that they will be so altered or that, if changes occur, each factor will be of equal significance. The intention in this section is to discuss the principles governing these changes.

The Return

Not all immigrants intend to remain in the host community for the rest of their lives. The health of individuals in the immigrant population may be modified by their length of stay in the new environment by the waning of previously acquired immunities which are no longer significant, and which are no longer subject to stimulation, in the new environment; these immunities may become important on the return of the immigrant to his native land where he will in some ways become an immigrant all over again. This waning of previously acquired immunity is seen most markedly in malaria and in immunity to some virus infections. The immigrant may also acquire a disease while he is in his new environment and later import this into his native land on his return. His length of stay and the extent of contact with the infective community would be important factors in governing whether or not he acquires this type of infection as well as consideration of his own individual resistance.

The children of an immigrant, if born in the host country, returning with their parents to the parents' native land would be strangers in more than one sense. Their acquired immunological pattern would be that of the country in which they had grown up and this would be far more important than any racial variation in resistance to infection. In addition they would be cultural strangers and would undergo the same cultural shock as is seen in children newly arriving in this country.

Changes in Population Structure

The arrival of a significant number of immigrants may affect the host community by altering the sex and age distribution of the combined population. In the early years of the arrival of an immigrant community there may be a preponderance of men who may be joined later by their families. In both these cases the age/sex distribution of the immigrant community would be different from that of the host community. With the arrival of the men's families there will be comparatively fewer very old people and initially comparatively fewer very young children in the immigrant population. The latter deficit would be made up within a few years, and there would then be a higher proportion of younger children in the immigrant community than in the host community, because the immigrant community would contain a higher proportion of women of child bearing age. This imbalance in the age/sex distribution of a population group has occurred many times in new housing estates and new towns.

The way in which the new population of the receptor area, now including indigenous and immigrant communities, changes depend on the number of immigrants involved, their numerical proportion compared to the indigenous community, to the age and sex distributions of the two communities and to any differences in fertility and reproduction rates which may be present between the two communities. It is quite impossible either to comment accurately or to forecast intelligently if the absolute numbers *and* the age and sex distribution of both indigenous and immigrant communities are not known. This is further discussed in Appendix III.

Summary

From the point of view of a receptor area, that is an area to which the immigrants are coming, the arrival of an immigrant population may cause one or more of the following factors to be of enhanced importance in the health of the new community, both corporate and individual.

1. A disease not generally present in the receptor country may be imported and this entails treatment for the person who has it. If it is transmissable it may be transmitted to others and these others may be fellow immigrants or members of the indigenous population.

2. Because of a different immunological background and sometimes because of a different racial background the immigrant may be more susceptible to particular diseases than a member of the indigenous community and measures will then be necessary to protect him against such diseases, to diagnose them as early as possible when they do occur and to treat them.

3. The natural history of the disease will be further influenced by the way of life of the immigrant, which is itself likely to be severely modified by the new environment.

4. Changes may occur in the reservoir of infection by the introduction of further cases or by a more susceptible immigrant population contracting infection after their arrival.

5. The immigrant is adapting into a new situation which is new immunologically and culturally, and possibly linguistically as well. Whatever the various factors are, one thing is certain and that is the new environment will be radically different from the one that the immigrant is used to and that adaptation will be enforced at a considerable rate. This will result in a greater degree of the normal stress of the daily life than the immigrant is accustomed to and greater than that endured by the average indigenous person. It is likely, therefore, that there will be an increased rate of ill health and incomplete adaptation to the new environment resulting from increased stress. The symptoms and the natural course of these stress disorders will be further modified by the particular racial and cultural background of the person concerned.

CHAPTER 3

CULTURE AND CUSTOM

Religion

MANY of the immigrant communities will have different religious beliefs from those of the host community and even when the basic religious faith is the same there may be considerable differences in practice. Jews have long been a migrant race and the fact that they are different and observe a separate faith has been observed for so long that they are accepted as part of the general community by all but a small minority in this country.

The majority of the immigrants coming into this country from other than European races and thereby readily noticeable as strangers come from the West Indies, Pakistan, India and Cyprus.

Nearly all Pakistanis are Moslem and although there are differences in faith between Moslems from different parts of the world, these differences are not great. The Islamic religion has a code of conduct which is detailed and covers the day to day life of its adherents. The religion of about 90 per cent of the population of India is Hinduism and this religion is of considerable antiquity. It is polytheistic (that is, identifying a number of deities), and shows much variation in different parts of India. The caste system is of great importance in Hinduism and there is a division into four main castes which are further sub-divided into sub-castes. Entry into a sub-caste is determined by birth and each caste and sub-caste has its pre-determined occupation and social position. These castes are inward looking and result in a fragmentation of society. In India the caste system is being steadily broken down against a considerable amount of resistance at times: it is still an important element in Indian social custom.

Hinduism is centred on the home and the congregational element in the worship is largely absent. Islam on the other hand has a strong congregational element as well as retaining a major role for individual observance.

28

Sikhs are members of a reformed movement within Hinduism which is monotheistic and rejects the caste system. It is a major Faith and there are about 10 million Sikhs, mostly in the Punjab region of India. Sikhism has a strong congregational element in its observance.

Cypriot immigrants are almost entirely of Greek origin and most are members of the Greek Orthodox Church. This branch of the Christian Religion stems from the early Christian Church and has very strong congregational and family elements as well as a patriarchal system. The social life of the Greek Cypriot is organized around his religious observances as is that of the Muslim, although in the Islamic faith the major role is taken by the men.

The religion of most West Indians is Christian. There is a correlation in the West Indies between a person's socio-economic status and the Church that person attends. There has been considerable differentiation between various sects and there are a number of sects which have a considerable following. The main Christian denominations (Anglican, Baptist, Methodist, Presbyterian, Roman Catholic, Moravian, Congregational) account for about three-quarters of church members and adherents, between 5 per cent and 10 per cent profess no religious attachment and the rest of the population follow one of a number of different sects— not all of them Christian. Religion, particularly when centred on the local church congregation, is a vital part of the life, especially in rural areas where most of the social life of the community is associated with the church and its services and festivals: a state of affairs resembling that found in rural England in the last generation and in some communities in the United Kingdom now.

Reference should be made to *Dark Strangers* by Sheila Patterson, for further details on this subject.

Religious prohibitions of certain foods

That Judaism prohibits the eating of pork is well known. Most Hindus and Sikhs are forbidden to eat beef, and pork is forbidden to all Moslems. There are also certain requirements regarding the manner in which the animal providing the meat is slaughtered and all meat may be refused if there is some doubt about the manner of slaughter. Prohibition of the meat of the animal applies also to animal products, including the fat of the animal and if it is thought that food has been cooked or fried with fat of a prohibited sort then the food will be refused. Some Hindus will decline all meat other than poultry and some will carry vegetarianism to the point at which eggs are refused, although milk and milk products are acceptable.

Fasts

The Christian fast time of Lent will be familiar, at least in concept, to most readers. The fast of Ramadan is the Moslem month of prayer and fasting, the fast being from dawn to dusk during which no food or drink is taken. Dawn and dusk are traditionally defined as the time when the difference between a white thread and a black thread is just distinguishable or just not distinguishable respectively. At the present day it is usual to define the starting and finishing times for each day's fast by reference to the clock and this is done by the religious leaders of the community. The month-long fast of Ramadan begins at the dawn following the first sighting of the new moon and ends on the evening on which the next new moon is sighted. In 1969 the fast will start in mid-November and as the dates of Ramadan are fixed by the lunar calender, the fast begins approximately ten days earlier each year.

Some of the effects of fasts and food prohibitions are considered further in other chapters.

Diet

By and large no general problems have been experienced with unavailability of particular items of food. Generally speaking, immigrant communities feel that they are able to buy such foods as are necessary for health, and in fact in many cases the standard of nutrition rises as some of these foods are more easily available and cheaper in this country. There are, of course, personal idiosyncrasies and isolated complaints of failure to buy a particular food, but generally no great difficulty seems to have been experienced. The Asian community is generally more affected by shortages of familiar foods and rather more of their customs concern food prohibitions than do those of other immigrant communities.

Some paediatricians have noted that out-patient clinic appointments and in-patient beds are more frequently occupied by immigrant children than otherwise would be expected in relation to their proportion in the community. This is probably because they are more frequently referred for expert advice. If a general practitioner is in doubt about a child he will tend to refer that child and such doubt may be increased by the difficulty of taking an adequate history of the illness. Of considerable importance, especially with reference to the child's diet, is the general immune state of an immigrant child which is usually less satisfactory than in the indigenous child: this is often a result of a less than adequate protein intake in the past. An immigrant child has to cope with viruses and also with bacteria of different antigenic strains than he or she has been accustomed to and this means that, particularly in the first year or two after entry to this country, the child is more liable to infections, which, particularly if the child is under-nourished, may become serious. The lack of protein intake may be exacerbated by a reluctance to put the child on an adequate protein diet soon after weaning.

In many of the countries from which immigrant children come, meat is relatively more expensive than in this country and the child may have had an inadequate intake of first class protein for some years. In addition, because of food prohibitions meat may not be given at all or in less than adequate amounts when the child arrives in this country: also, because of the shortage of familiar cereals which have provided protein in the past, intake of this second class protein may be reduced and the nutritional state made worse than before immigration. Generally the men are more amenable to advice about diet, whereas the women, if of a tenacious frame of mind, may be very resistant to new ideas. These new ideas will be best introduced by members of the same community, perhaps with a little initial stimulus. The child who is being weaned may also experience a shortage of first class protein due to food prohibitions and lack of knowledge about what foods in the permitted range are available. It is, again, the strict non-meat eater rather than those with prohibitions about certain meats who will give rise to most of the difficulties of this sort.

Pregnant and nursing mothers need an additional protein intake. They may be reluctant to meet this need for the reasons discussed above and attention should be directed to this point in the ante-natal clinic and by the health visitor visiting the new infant and mother.

Purdah

This will be seen in Muslim communities and, particularly in newly arrived immigrants, Purdah may cause some complications. In clinics where the obstetrician happens to be a man there may be some reluctance to present for examination, but there is considerable variation from one Muslim community to another. Generally this reluctance becomes quickly modified and as the immigrant community becomes established, it becomes much less of a difficulty. However, many ante-natal and midwifery units have male and female medical staff and this difficulty will not generally be insurmountable.

A very small number of women may be reluctant even to leave their homes to come to a clinic. Such occurrences are rare and are best dealt with as individual cases, and it is generally not necessary to make special provision for these. It has been found that the local taxi service is frequently used by Muslim immigrants and has proved extremely useful in enabling them to attend clinics.

The general beliefs surrounding the custom of Purdah may severely modify the patient's own attitude to ante-natal and post-natal clinics, but generally speaking there will be little in the way of difficulty with regard to attendance at an ante-natal clinic. The general background of the immigrant should however be kept in mind by the midwife and health visitor so that difficulties may be dealt with while they are potential rather than actual. Because of their beliefs the patients may in fact feel more uneasy about being examined by a male doctor from their own country than they would on being examined by a male European doctor. The matter of Purdah could become important if medical aid had to be urgently sought for a child where the mother was alone in the house and unwilling to leave it because of restrictions of Purdah. Experience has shown that this attitude, although it has on occasions shown itself, is extremely rare and most likely to occur in the very recently arrived immigrant. The local authority ante-natal and infant welfare clinics do a great deal in providing the means for social contact between women immigrants, and this is of particular importance where women come from communities where it is not the custom of women to leave the house a great deal. It is in these circumstances that the provision of facilities for women to meet, talk and exchange gossip and advice is of great importance and, if information is made available when and where required, a great deal of good preventive medicine may be done. In this respect almost any excuse for holding a clinic will do.

Because they are, in general, less used to having to make decisions for their family, a number of immigrant mothers may not call in medical aid when it is required by themselves or their children, but will wait until the man of the house, or a male relative, can be found or returns home from work. In addition both parents may, because they are unfamiliar with the ready provision of medical aid, call for the doctor late in the course of the illness and may also ignore significant symptoms. This will usually not be too serious in the adult but in the child may be disastrous.

Marriage and Divorce

The average Asian wife is very much dependent upon her husband and this is particularly so in the case of the Muslim woman. Apart from a few decisions about her baby's care she does not make independent decisions and for most things she has to have her husband's approval. In many matters health education may be initiated through the husband, (for example, family planning). In the case of the West Indian immigrants the women are much more independent and have a considerable say in the running of the family's affairs. There will be considerable variations between members of the same race and it is not wise to proceed unchecked from a generalization to assumptions about a particular person.

Assumptions and assertions concerning 'they' or 'them' are as frequently as inaccurate as they are unwarranted. To take a

C

specific example from a custom which has been frequently commented upon: namely the custom of some West Indian married couples to get married sometime during their life together rather than at the beginning. A number of unhelpful deductions have been made on this point. The most important factor in the health of the family is whether the marriage is stable rather than whether it is legal. (Legal, that is, from the point of view of having entered into a state of legal matrimony—bigamy would be generally regarded as unstable). If the union is a stable one and the family is well-founded, questions as to whether the man and wife are legally married are irrelevant—apart from consideration of some family and other allowances: it is not the prerogative of the health worker to intervene or advise in any way in this matter. The question of whether or not the children are legally illegitimate, whilst irrelevant in the context of the particular family, may be of concern in the context of the wider community. There has in most areas where West Indian immigrants have become settled and established been a change in attitude in this matter—but whether due to integration with the local English customs or whether influenced by such considerations as family and other allowances, is not precisely clear.

Different communities have different views of marriage and this applies to different indigenous communities in this country as much as it does to the various immigrant communities. The health worker should never be seen to stand in judgment upon these matters but, on the other hand, he or she should not ignore differences and treat them as if they did not exist. Differences in customs should be treated for what they are: merely differences in customs rather than differences in degrees of moral excellence. In following this exhortation, care must be taken not to become unbalanced in the opposite direction. Abnormal and unusual conduct may not simply be unEnglish—it may be abnormal as well.

In some communities divorce is much easier than it is under the general law of this country, but problems arising from this have not yet become apparent. If they did appear, the health worker should refer such matters to the proper authorities and these proper authorities would certainly include the leaders of the particular immigrant community. In theory, polygamy might present some problems in immigrant Muslim households, but again so far this has been a theoretical consideration rather than a practical one. The practice of having more than one wife is looked upon with disfavour by many Muslims today.

Selection of Suitors

According to custom Asian women may have their husbands chosen for them by their parents. It is likely, however, that this state of affairs will be unacceptable to the children of these immigrant families who have grown up in this country and have absorbed English ways along with their English education. Of considerable concern to members of the Pakistani community in this country is the difficulty of finding suitors for their daughters. It is probable that in the not too distant future their daughters will wish to find their own suitors and this will give rise to considerable stresses within the immigrant families. It is certain that the Asian girl teenager will not be content to remain in the house as her mother was brought up to do and any change will be accelerated when the girl goes out to work and becomes financially independent. She will then most certainly no longer wish to rely on the men of the household to make her decisions for her.

Adolescence

The storms of adolescence are not quite so much in evidence in eastern culture as they are in this country, but it is likely that they may well become considerably more apparent in the generation now attending school. It may well be that the health worker has a part to play in the future here although initially such a part will be a small one, as he or she would quite rightly be regarded as a 'foreigner'. For the health visitor or health auxillary who is of the same race as the particular immigrant group, much opportunity for giving advice is likely to occur in the future on this subject and this is likely to be a most worthwhile occupation, although not an easy one. There are bound to be considerable changes in the way of life of the first generation descendants of immigrants, par-ticularly those from Asian families. If anything can be done to meet the strain resulting from these changes the effort should certainly be made. Outside the province of this particular work, but nevertheless a point worthy of note, is that there will be problems of integration in reverse when children of immigrant parents educated in this country return to their own countries where local custom may be considerably different.

Illegitimate births

Considerable difficulties are caused particularly in Asian households by a daughter having an illegitimate child. In a Muslim community this would be regarded as an exceptionally serious matter and could lead to the girl being disowned by her family. The child would be quite unacceptable and would have to be taken into the care of the local authority, who would also probably have to care for the girl as well. It has been known for girls of all races to become pregnant by reason of a complete lack of knowledge of 'the facts of life'. Asian girls brought up in restricted communities may, when they come to this country with their parents, be even more restricted as the only female relative around is the mother who may fail to give any information at all. This is not a problem which can be dealt with by a health education campaign, but will need attention by those responsible for the care of the community: the community leaders would seem to be the most fitted for this, but the problem may have to be put to them as, because they themselves do not lead such a restricted life, they may be unaware of the difficulties.

Names

The system of naming causes considerable confusion in Western European minds which have long been accustomed to follow a system which has become confused with the pre-ordained order of things. Way back in the days of 1066 and all that, most people had only one name to which was sometimes added, to make identification easier, a description of the occupation and sometimes a reference to the name of the person's father. In this country, during the fourteenth century and coinciding with movement of population to the towns, a person was often named after his place of birth. In later years these systems were gradually adopted officially and the present system of surnames grew up. In communities in rural areas many names became modified by the addition of a nickname and these sometimes became substituted for the original surnames. With the increasing movement of the population and the need for identification of the individual, the present system of surnames and forenames became established: with the registration of births and deaths and the founding of the Registrar General's Office in the middle of the nineteenth century possession of a surname and forename became a social necessity.

Not all countries follow this practice or observe the order in which European names are put. For example—if Chiang Kai Shek attends a hospital, he must first register: he is likely to have his case notes inscribed SHEK, Chiang Kai: they should be labelled CHIANG, Kai Shek.

Because the names of West Indian immigrants follow the pattern common here and in America and are indistinguishable from English names, little difficulty is caused. It is the system of Asian names which has given rise to the greatest difficulty. A number of people are accustomed to a Sikh being known as Mr Singh: this is in fact incorrect although it is commonly used and has been adopted by many immigrant Sikhs. The word SINGH is a title and denotes a male Sikh, just as KAUR denotes a female Sikh. Moslem women often have the title BEGUM as a first or second name: KHANUM is used less frequently in the same way. SHEIK, KHAN and MALIK are used in the same way by Muslim men: they are courtesy titles but are also used as names.

To quote from an example given by Dr Anand in his article in the *Medical Officer* of 22nd March 1968 and to which reference may be made: when Joginder Singh Gill arrives in Britain his passport may bear the legend 'Joginder Singh, son of Amirt Singh'. His national insurance card and his national health service card will therefore bear the name 'Joginder Singh'. When his wife arrives, her passport may bear the name 'Sukhdev Kaur'. When the couple's first daughter is born, she may be registered as Hardev Kaur. If the wife visits hospital and her husband accompanies her to translate, she may well be registered as 'SINGH,

Sukhdev' or even as 'SINGH, Kaur'. When the midwife notifies the birth of the daughter, she may write the name as 'Hardev Singh' and 'Hardev Kaur' or 'Hardev Kaur Singh'. When the child is at school and reference is made to clinic and hospital records there may be apparently three children involved and not one. Fortunately most immigrants have become aware of the local system of names fairly rapidly and have learned to stick to one 'surname'.

It is better to use the term 'forename' or 'given name' rather than Christian name: the term 'surname' is usually understood, especially if it is amplified by 'or family name'. This will tend to avoid such apparent confusions as 'Christian name—Mohammed'.

Health Departments, Hospitals, Education Departments, local offices of Government Ministries are advised to provide their reception clerks with two questions printed in English, Urdu, Punjabi and Hindi: namely—

1. What is your name (family name)?
2. What are your forenames (given names, Baptismal names)?

Frequently the newly arrived immigrant is requested to produce his or her passport in order to ascertain the correct name. Often the immigrant speaking little English will produce the passport unasked as a means of identification. There are a number of dangers in this. The authorities who completed the passport may not follow the same system of naming and the passport may not bear exactly the same name as used by the immigrant and in addition the demand for the passport may cause resentment. It should be noted that because of the lack of a system of birth registration and the associated issue of a birth certificate, the passport of the parent is not a reliable guide to the age of his children. It should be remembered that the immigrant is not trying to deceive, to hide his family name or to be obtuse: he is not accustomed to the use of names in the manner practised in this country and may not fully understand the questions put to him.

The name system employed by Cypriots often causes some confusion as the Christian name of the father is often used as the surname of the child. Also the age of the child is counted as one more than the chronological age and this may lead to mutual suspicion arising from mutual incomprehension.

The Age of children

The lack of a system of birth registration in many countries and the consequent lack of birth certificates gives rise to considerable difficulty as the immigrant may not remember exactly how old his children are and may in the heat of the moment and under the pressure of officialdom asking all manner of apparently unrelated questions, miscalculate. (This miscalculation has been committed by a multitude of English fathers under the same circumstances). The passport is little help as the same miscalculation may have occurred then: it may have been completed incorrectly by the applicant or the issuing authorities and in any case anyone can see what size the child is and the exact age is not all that important—a viewpoint which may be regretted by the interviewer but is nevertheless understandable. If the age given appears to be seriously inaccurate and it is not possible to get a reasonably accurate assessment because the child is either abnormally small or appears developed far beyond his years, X-ray examination of the growing ends of the bones, generally the knees and wrists, is helpful: obviously this is only to be done under medical supervision. It is only necessary in the selected case.

Clothing

Generally speaking the clothing of immigrants who come from warmer countries tends to be thin and multi-layered. This is fairly satisfactory if the weather is warm but it is extremely unsatisfactory in winter and clear advice needs to be given with regard to the clothing of infants and school children. Cold injury of the new-born is a hazard which must be guarded against by giving advice and instruction before the event and the child born to the newly arrived mother from a warm climate should be regarded as being at special risk. It is also possible to provide too much clothing and an over-wrapped baby in an over-heated room is equally at risk. Advice must be directed at producing the desirable rather than a change from the undesirable. The changeability of the English climate is something to which the indigenous have become at least partially accustomed: the immigrant is probably used to the changing seasons but will not be used to having them all at once.

The school child may be inadequately clothed. The Asian girl clad in thin trousers and who may have little between them and herself will be extremely cold in winter and this will considerably reduce interest in school and will lower bodily resistance so that upper respiratory infections in particular will become too common a cause of school absence—and may proceed to more serious complications. Now that the Asian community is becoming more established, these dangers are well known to the community and are usually passed on to new arrivals. They can and do still occur, however, and will be seen by teachers teaching newly arrived immigrant children.

The winter vests and long-legged pants as produced for men have been adopted with enthusiasm by some Asian women and when worn under their customary dress could hardly be bettered. Clothing for women and children if of the cheapest sort is often inadequate both as to quality and to durability: advice spread through the immigrants own community will be the most appropriate method of dealing with this, but its diffusion may need a start from whoever may have the opportunity. The men are generally more protected and, because they are accustomed to dress in the same manner as the indigenous male, are not often more affected by the cold. They can, and do, easily add another layer.

Heating

There is a tendency amongst immigrant families to buy the cheapest heating available. This is partly due to a wish to economize on heating the house and also to a lack of knowledge of the ways of and the necessity for heating a house in an English winter. Paraffin heaters are in common use and these may be old and of a dangerous pattern. Furthermore an immigrant family may be uncertain as to the correct way of operating the paraffin heater and may fill it while it is lit, use it without ventilation or leave it in a room with young children. In spite of the publicity about the dangers of certain paraffin heaters which has had considerable effect in the incidence of accidents with heaters in the indigenous community, fires due to paraffin heaters being upset are still common in the immigrant community. This type of heater is more popular among the West Indians than among the Asians who generally prefer an open type fire which may be unguarded. Selection of the correct forms of heating and the proper guarding of open fires, particularly in immigrant communities, is still a most important part of general health education.

The long flowing type of dress such as the sari can be a considerable personal risk if there is an open fire and generally speaking any open fire should be guarded by an *adequate* guard.

The health or the social worker on every visit to the house should watch out for this and advise when necessary. Like most acts of health education, a short piece of advice simply put and simply explained is effective: long and involved explanations laced with anecdotes are seldom heeded.

Hygiene and Sanitation

In a number of the 'developing' countries a notable feature of the transition from a rural environment to an urban one is the considerable increase in the incidence of gastro-intestinal diseases. The increase in these diseases is consequent on the problem of disposing of human excreta and refuse and was a main concern in the public health in this country in the eighteenth and nineteenth centuries. Provision of a water supply inside the house, provision of a bathroom, the existence of water-borne sanitation and a refuse collection and disposal service are things that we now take for granted in this country. Difficulty is often experienced by a newly arrived immigrant who is unfamiliar with these amenities and the way in which they work and this unfamiliarity is most commonly seen in women and children arriving in the country straight from a rural community. The men are more travelled and have seen all these things before: to a person who has seldom left her own village and has now come several thousand miles in a day or less to a strange country, climate and custom, the change is a frightening one.

Difficulty can be experienced in persuading mothers to train their young children to conform to acceptable sanitary habits. A considerable amount has been written on this subject and a great deal of it has been exaggerated, but nevertheless there is a considerable need for instruction in the use of all sanitary amenities, in disposal of refuse and in general cleanliness in food production. The impetus for such education can be given by the health visitor and carried on by the more knowledgeable and more firmly established members of the local immigrant community. A problem may arise with immigrants who firmly believe in the necessity of washing in running water and use running water to cleanse the perineum after defaecation rather than toilet paper. This may involve the provision of showers and a bidet in addition to the water closet. While not suggesting that major acts of sanitary reconstruction be done in houses occupied by immigrants, nevertheless this is a point which should be considered by those responsible for housing, and if housing is being constructed which may be used by a particular community, then the habits of that community should at least be considered by those responsible for the planning. The possibility, for example, for the easy installation of a bidet at the tenant's expense could be incorporated into housing design without much trouble. What should be aimed at is not the free provision of all these things but that a person might be able to obtain for himself by his own efforts what could be reasonably made available.

Children being more adaptable, do not cause quite so much of a problem: nevertheless a newly arrived school-child should be taught how the 'plumbing' works as a piece of initial school instruction, and it is right and proper that this should be done.

Instruction is frequently needed in basic sanitation and household cleanliness, not because an immigrant community is less clean than the indigenous one, but because they are used to different methods of cleaning and these methods may be neither applicable nor obtainable in this country. For example, cleaning of the feeding bottle with Vim has been noted: this is hardly surprising if both the feeding bottle and the profusion of cleansing agents available in the corner shop are both completely new to the immigrant mother.

General instruction may be indicated in households where there is a common towel for the whole family and also in the use of the individual handkerchief, or better still in the use of paper handkerchiefs properly disposed of.

The advantages of the automatic launderette is apparent to the immigrant community as much as it is to the indigenous one, and, even if the women are unable for reasons of custom, to visit the launderette with the washing, they are able to send the children. The benefits of frequent washing of clothes and bedding are generally apparent but may need some amplification. The washing of pots and pans and dishes may be deficient and assistance may be needed in deciding which cleaning agent to use. In houses let in multiple occupation where, particularly, the unaccompanied Asian male lives, there may be a considerable lack of hygiene in the preparation of food and cleansing of cooking and eating utensils, and while the adult male's stomach may have considerable resistance to the assaults of sub-acute doses of toxins, nevertheless there is a fruitful field here for health education. The health visitor is unlikely to visit these households very frequently but the housing inspector, public health inspector and sometimes the infectious diseases inspector or nurse may well find the opportunity and need for health education here.

The disposal of the dead

All residents in the country are liable to the laws of the country. Certification, registration and, if appropriate, a report to the Coroner will follow according to common practice. Disposal of the dead in an unhealthy or unseemly manner is prohibited by the law: there are no rites or rituals of any immigrant group which would be liable to offend either against the public health or normal custom.

Most readers in this country will be familiar with the rites and customs of the various Christian Churches. The following is given for information.

Cremation is not practised by Muslims. The body is wrapped in three pieces of cloth, usually white, and is buried, usually without a coffin, in a niche cut into the side of the grave, so that when the grave is filled, the earth does not rest on the body. The grave must be orientated so that the face of the deceased is towards Mecca.

Buddhists often cremate the body, but there is no rigid practice in this. The headstone, whether the body or the ashes are buried, must have on it the Buddhist symbol.

Cremation is the orthodox method of disposal of the body among Hindus. It is important that the proper rites be observed and if this is not possible, for example in a death at sea, they are performed as soon as possible afterwards. Certain ceremonies are also necessary on the anniversaries of the death. It is often desired that the ashes or part of them, be sent to relatives in India so that they may be scattered on the River Ganges.

If it is desired that a body be removed out of England, then the Coroner within whose jurisdiction the body lies must be informed. The Coroner may, after proper enquiries, issue a certificate and the body may not be removed from the country until this has been done. Normally the enquiries take at least four days. The importation of a body into a country is the concern of that country, not the country from which the body comes and Governments will make regulations concerning the requirements which have to be met.

CHAPTER 4

IMMIGRANTS AND THE LAW

THE LAWS of the United Kingdom apply equally to all citizens whether immigrant or indigenous: there are, however, some laws which apply particularly to immigrants. The two Commonwealth Immigration Acts and the various Acts governing Aliens are examples of these: the Race Relations Act does not refer specifically to immigrants except in one small exemption with regard to restriction of employment on grounds of race or colour. There has been considerable confusion on the content and scope of legislation particularly applicable to immigrants and much of this springs from the fact that 'Immigrant' has become an emotive word in recent years: much misquoting of the relevant Acts has occurred with the presentation of doubtful truths under the misnomer of 'statistics'. The intention of this section is to present the important facts about the law and a little of the background to them.

Aliens

An alien is a person who is a national of a country other than the United Kingdom, or is a person who is stateless, and who is not a citizen of a Commonwealth country.

The law governing the entry and movement of aliens is complex. In general, however, an alien may not enter this country without a visa and this is granted only on specific conditions. The visa is valid for a limited time, and the maximum length of stay permitted would usually be twelve months. The purpose of entry must be stated and this is one of the factors controlling whether or not a visa is granted. Visitors would not usually have much trouble in getting a visa as tourists, or to visit relatives already in this country: students would usually get a visa provided that their place of study was already fixed: entry for work would be more difficult and would depend on the particular skills of the alien and whether or not there was a particular job available. An alien may not take up employment in this country unless the visa permits him or her to do so, neither may aliens change their employment without authority from the Home Office. All aliens are registered and the police of the area in which the alien lives have details of the visa, address, work etc. An alien is required to inform the police of a change of address.

An alien may apply for extension of his visa and this would generally be granted unless there was some reason why it should not be. The police usually visit an alien a month or so before his visa expires to ensure that the alien is aware that reapplication is necessary. The Home Office may, after a series of applications for renewal of a visa, decide that no further applications are necessary and the visa then becomes an unrestricted one: the holder remains an alien but is exempted from re-applying periodically for renewal of his visa.

Immigration from Commonwealth Countries and the Commonwealth Immigration Acts

Up to 1962 all Commonwealth citizens were entitled to enter the United Kingdom without restriction: this right of free entry had been exercised for many years but it was only from the beginning of the 1950's onwards that a substantial number of people from the Commonwealth began to settle in Britain. The following figures show the net intake of Commonwealth citizens from the Caribbean, Asia, East and West Africa and the Mediterranean from the beginning of 1955 to the middle of 1962:

1955	42,700
1956	46,850
1957	42,400
1958	29,850
1959	21,600
1960	57,700
1961	136,400
1962	94,900 (For the first six months)

Restriction on the number of immigrants entering from Commonwealth countries was introduced by the 1962 Commonwealth Immigrants Act because the Government believed that the number of immigrants then entering the country was too great and outran the capacity of the country to absorb them. Section 2 of the 1962 Act gave an immigration officer power to refuse admission, to admit subject to a condition restricting the period of stay or to admit with or without a condition restricting freedom to take employment. The restrictions mainly concerned those Commonwealth citizens who wished to settle and to work in the United Kingdom, and for this a Ministry of Labour voucher had to be obtained. There were three categories of vouchers, known as A, B and C.

Category A Vouchers were issued upon application by employers in this country who had a specific job to offer a specific Commonwealth citizen.

Category B Vouchers were issued upon application by the Commonwealth citizen without a specific job to come to but with certain special qualifications—for example, nurses, teachers, doctors etc.

A *Category C* Voucher was for all other categories.

Applications in Categories 'A' and 'B' were given priority over Category 'C'. In the first two years following the passing of this Act, a number of vouchers in Categories 'A' and 'B' were not taken up but from September 1964 onwards the two priority classes (Categories 'A' and 'B') took up the whole issue of four hundred vouchers per week. By the middle of 1965 a waiting list of 300,000 applicants had grown up in Category 'C'. Up to August 1965 vouchers were issued at the rate of 400 a week, i.e. 20,800 a year. From August 1965 the rate of issue of vouchers was set at 8,500 a year; this figure included 1,000 vouchers which were, as a temporary measure, allocated to citizens of Malta who satisfied the conditions of the voucher scheme. There was a further proviso that not more than fifteen per cent of vouchers issued in Category 'A' would go to any one Commonwealth country in order to share out the available vouchers between different Commonwealth countries.

The 1962 Act gave an absolute right of entry to the wife and to any child under sixteen of a Commonwealth citizen who is travelling with them to the United Kingdom (in which case he would be a voucher holder) or who is already resident here. Other categories of dependants were, in practice, admitted without vouchers under the discretionary powers given to the Immigration Officers: these were:

(a) a child under sixteen coming to join a close relative, other than a parent.

(b) a son or daughter aged sixteen but under eighteen coming with, or to join a parent.

(c) the fiancée or common law wife of a man settled here.

(d) the widowed mother or elderly parents of a person settled here.

Bona fide students and visitors were freely admitted and arrangements were made for any Commonwealth citizens seeking admission without a voucher to apply for an entry certificate before leaving their homes, to make reasonably sure of being admitted on arrival. In 1963, 1964 and 1965 there was a marked reduction in the number of voucher holders admitted but this was counter-balanced by an increase in the number of dependants accompanying or joining the head of the family.

There is a considerable to and fro movement of citizens of Canada, Australia and New Zealand and of citizens from other Commonwealth countries. The total number leaving the country is a considerable proportion of the total entering the country in the same year. The following figures illustrate this point:

A. Citizens of Canada, Australia or New Zealand (1963–65)

Numbers Admitted	1963	1964	1965
(a) Visitors	130,625	151,737	76,680
(b) Students	2,114	2,073	696
(c) Voucher Holders	1,447	817	321
(d) Others (mainly dependants)	2,288	2,243	1,011
(e) Remainder (mainly returning students)	51,093	55,869	25,758
Total admitted	187,567	212,739	104,466
Total embarked	178,616	199,357	88,752

B. Citizens from other Commonwealth Countries and Dependent Territories (1963-65)

Numbers Admitted	1963	1964	1965
(a) Visitors	57,365	62,825	25,733
(b) Students	16,370	18,044	4,581
(c) Voucher Holders	28,678	13,888	6,771
(d) Others (mainly dependants)	27,393	38,952	19,849
(e) Remainder (mainly returning students)	48,364	60,153	27,989
Total admitted	178,170	193,862	84,923
Total embarked	121,121	131,745	51,540
Net balance	57,049	62,117	33,383

C. Citizens of Canada, Australia or New Zealand (1966-67)

	1966	1967
Total immigrants admitted	35,400	45,200
Total emigrants embarked	169,900	159,500
Balance	(−) 127,500	(−) 114,300

D. Citizens from other Commonwealth Countries and Dependent Territories (1966-67)

	1966	1967
Total immigrants admitted	74,000	84,200
Total emigrants embarked	40,100	38,800
Balance	(+) 33,900	(+) 45,400

	1967
Admitted and embarking aliens. Net balance	(+) 27,500

Immigrant—intending to reside in U.K. for at least a year.
Emigrant—intending to reside in country of destination for at least a year.

In 1965 a review was made of the application of the 1962 Commonwealth Immigration Act: no changes were made in the statutory right of a wife of an immigrant and his children under sixteen to accompany or follow him into the country but, with a view to preventing evasion of the 1962 Act, Immigration Officers

D

were instructed to apply stricter tests of eligibility which would take into account the production of entry certificates or other appropriate documents establishing the identity of the would-be entrant. The practice of admitting freely children aged 16–18 years coming to join one or both parents was withdrawn except in special cases, and, similarly, the concession applying to children under sixteen joining a relative other than a parent was withdrawn as a considerable number of immigrants were arriving at or near school age simply to enter employment in this country without having to wait for a voucher. The Government continued to welcome Commonwealth citizens entering this country on holiday, on social or business visits or to follow courses of study; but in order to prevent people admitted on the pretext of a visit or a course of study from obtaining permanent settlement, the practice of admitting students and others for limited periods, to be extended if necessary was continued. Additional powers were taken in 1965 so that, at the discretion of Immigration Authorities, any immigrant, including dependants, might be medically examined at the point of entry and could be required as a condition of entry to report to the Medical Officer of Health of the place of his destination with a view to necessary medical treatment being arranged. No powers, however, were taken to refuse entry on medical grounds to entitled dependants.

In the White Paper presented to Parliament in August 1965, a large section was devoted to integration of Commonwealth immigrants into the society and economy of the country. It was recognized that the concentration of immigrants in certain urban areas where social services were already under strain had arisen largely because of the opportunities for work in these areas. The rapid increase in population consequent on migration into these areas from within the country as well as from overseas stretched the already strained social services, particularly in Housing and Education, towards breaking point. It was felt that special treatment should not be given to immigrants with regard to housing and that the sole test for action in the housing field would be the quality and nature of the housing need without distinctions based on the origin of those in need. In education the difficulty arising from the arrival of immigrant children knowing little or no

English was noted: the White Paper advised that special arrangements must be made to teach English and to bring these children
up to the general standards achieved by children of the same age
group. To do this, and to effect the integration of children more
readily, the proportion of immigrant children in a school should
not rise too high. The circular by the Department of Education
and Science on 14th June 1965 suggested that one-third of
immigrant children should be the maximum normally acceptable
in a school. Local Education Authorities were advised to arrange
for the dispersal of immigrant children over a greater number of
schools in order to avoid undue concentration in any particular
school. The circular also proposed that measures for training
immigrant teachers should begin as soon as possible.

The White Paper noted that the great majority of immigrants
were fully employed and working in a wide range of occupations
but nevertheless there were indications of persisting discrimination. In Employment Exchanges it was ruled that any employer
attaching discriminatory conditions on grounds of race was not to
be assisted by Exchanges to fill vacancies. In practice, if an
employer imposes such discriminatory conditions, a senior officer
of the Employment Exchange will visit him and endeavour to
persuade him against this course. This persuasion is usually
successful but if the employer insists in attaching such conditions,
then the Government Order operates and an employer is not
assisted to fill vacancies by the Exchange.

The White Paper recognized the importance of the detection of
imported disease with particular reference to the detection and
prevention of tuberculosis. It noted that there was a considerable
problem of communication between Health Departments and
newly arrived immigrants and recommended that much could be
done by the employment of suitable members of immigrant
communities as health visitors, midwives, nurses etc. The formation of the National Council for Commonwealth Immigrants was
foreshadowed by the White Paper and this Council was intended
to take over and to co-ordinate the work of a number of voluntary
bodies concerned with Commonwealth immigrants.

The 1962 Act did not apply to a person born in the United
Kingdom or to a person holding a United Kingdom passport and

being a citizen of the United Kingdom Colonies. Because a considerable number of Commonwealth citizens held United Kingdom passports or were entitled under various agreements with territories formerly under British rule to apply for and be issued with United Kingdom passports it was felt that, if a considerable number of Commonwealth citizens in this category entered the United Kingdom at any one time, an unbearable strain would be placed upon the social services in the 'reception' areas. Because of political pressures at that time on Kenyan Asians who had not taken Kenyan Citizenship but had retained their Citizenship of the United Kingdom and Colonies (and thus the right of entry into the United Kingdom as holders of a United Kingdom passport), the numbers of Kenyan Asians entering this country had begun to rise. Comment on this and the resulting public debate caused a rapid increase in the number entering as those who had been considering such a move now hastened to achieve it before restrictions were introduced. The 1968 Immigration Act was therefore debated against the background of a specific problem and a rapidly increasing migration from a particular area and was introduced and passed into law with a significant amount of haste.

The 1968 Commonwealth Immigration Act restricted the definition of 'Citizen of the United Kingdom and Colonies' by inserting the following additional conditions: namely, that the person or at least one of his parents or grandparents:—

was born in the United Kingdom

or is or was a person naturalized in the United Kingdom

or became a citizen of the United Kingdom and Colonies by being adopted in the United Kingdom

or became such a citizen by being registered under the British Nationality Acts of 1948 or 1964.

The two Immigration Acts do not make easy reading; the effect of the 1968 Act can be summarized as placing restriction on the entry of immigrants who although citizens of the United Kingdom and Colonies were not themselves born in the United Kingdom or who are not the descendants of the first or second generation of persons who were born or naturalized in the United Kingdom.

Although much of the publicity surrounding this Act referred specifically to the Commonwealth Citizens originating in India and resident in Kenya who, under the provisions of the Kenya Independence Bill, were able to apply for United Kingdom Passports as Citizens of the United Kingdom and Colonies, these Commonwealth citizens did not by any means form the majority of those affected by the 1968 Act.

The aim of both Commonwealth Immigration Acts is that the influx of Commonwealth immigrants should be restricted to a point at which the net intake can be accommodated by the Social Services of the areas to which they are going. The number of Commonwealth immigrants now entering this country as voucher holders is small but recently a considerable number of dependants have joined the voucher holders already here. It seems that this was a temporary phenomenon and the number of new arrivals, including dependants is now decreasing again.

In Canada, Australia and New Zealand there is a general shortage of labour and the number of immigrants from these Commonwealth countries has been comparatively small: the effect of the restriction of immigrants has been largely felt by those Commonwealth countries where there is considerable unemployment and these are also countries with populations of Asian or African descent, and thus the question of colour has thus become inextricably bound up with the matter. An influx of the same proportions of workers and their families from any country or from the next county would have overloaded the social services in the receptor area by virtue of the sudden increase of population although the details of the effects of the overloading would not be exactly the same.

Generally speaking, in the years since 1955 immigrant workers arrived at first on their own and caused little effect on any pre-existing shortages in schools and hospital services: the initial effect on the housing in areas in which there was a housing shortage was to increase the shortage somewhat (although not to the extent which would have occurred had family groups been arriving together) and to give rise to the particular problems concerned with multiple occupancy. The later arrival of families resulted in a severe strain on housing suitable for family occupancy and on schools and the hospital services concerned with family needs. It is probable that, because the initial impact of the immigrant community on the health, welfare and educational services was comparatively slight, by virtue of the disproportionate number of adult males, the future needs were grossly underestimated.

The barriers of language and social class have tended to delay both the recognition of the problems and the application of solutions and as any solution needs to be constantly modified in accordance with a 'feed-back' of information on the changing situation, barriers of communication cause further delay by the continuation of out-of-date solutions to problems which no longer apply.

The most important effect of colour has been to render a section of the community readily noticeable. The existence of a readily distinguishable group which either does not conform, or can be pointed out with real or apparent justification as not conforming, to the popular concept of correct 'behaviour' forms the basis of discrimination. Discrimination against one person by another or by one group against another is a common occurrence and the grounds on which the discrimination is made are legion. If there are shortages in the social services or employment the association of an easily identifiable minority with such shortages is readily made and this forms the basis of the justification for discrimination: the important detail is that the discrimination precedes the justification and this is an indication that one must look elsewhere for the aetiology of the discrimination.

It has recently been considered that discrimination on the grounds of race or colour was increasing and could become a serious problem unless the hands of those who were concerned with the prevention of this type of conflict were strengthened. With this aim in view the Race Relations Bill was conceived and finally delivered after a somewhat protracted labour.

The Race Relations Act of 1968 makes certain forms of discrimination unlawful and provides for a conciliation service if such discrimination is established. Only if conciliation fails and the offender is apparently determined to repeat the unlawful conduct are the courts brought into the matter: if the courts are involved they may make an order or injunction restraining the offender from certain specified conduct in the future and if such conduct is repeated then this becomes a breach of a court order and action is taken by the courts.

The Act applies if unlawful discrimination is applied on the grounds and in the particular areas defined in the Act. The Act defines discrimination as 'less favourable treatment than would be given to other persons' and discrimination occurs if this less favourable treatment is applied on grounds of colour, race, ethnic or national origins. Segregating a person from another on these grounds would amount to discrimination.

Discrimination is unlawful if it occurs in the provision of goods, admission to a place to which the public has access, facilities in respect of banking, insurance and credit, provision of education and training, recreation, refreshment, transport and travel and the services of any business, profession, trade, local or other public authority. It is also unlawful in regard to employment if employment is refused completely or is offered under conditions of service different from those normally offered or if dismissal from that employment differs from that normally applicable. Trade Unions and employers or trade organizations may not discriminate on the grounds mentioned above by refusing membership, rights and privileges or benefits. It is unlawful to discriminate on these grounds in the disposal of land, housing and business premises either by refusing to sell, applying special conditions or preventing or seeking to prevent a person from acquiring land, housing accommodation or business premises. It is unlawful also to publish an advertisement indicating the intention to discriminate, although there are exceptions to this with regard to advertisements for Commonwealth citizens to be employed either in Great Britain or outside it.

There are a number of other exemptions to the Act. With regard to hotels, boarding houses etc. exemption from the provisions of the Act is obtained if the landlord or a member of his own household resides on the premises *and* there are not normally more than two households plus the landlord's household resident *or* when there is accommodation for not more than twelve people (this figure is reduced to six after the Act has been in force for two years). Employers employing less than twenty-five employees are exempted for the first two years of the Act and those with less than ten employees for the next two years. An employer may discriminate on grounds of good faith if this is done to preserve or restore a balance of persons of different racial groups, but this does not apply to employees born in Great Britain or mainly or wholly educated in Great Britain: this particular exemption is applicable only to immigrants in the exact sense of the word and may not be applied indiscriminately on grounds of colour or race. Race can be a qualification for a particular job (e.g. a waiter in a Chinese restaurant) and as such is exempted from the application of the Act.

Residential accommodation, if sold wholly privately and if occupied wholly by the vendor, is exempted from the provisions of the Act.

Incitement to discriminate is unlawful under the Race Relations Act: incitement to racial hatred is an offence under the criminal law. It should be clearly understood that the Race Relations Act is primarily concerned with the prevention of discrimination on the grounds covered by the Act, by conciliation in private, when investigation (also in private) has indicated that unlawful discrimination has occurred. Investigation and conciliation are the function of the Race Relations Board and its regional Conciliation Committees: the courts are involved only if conciliation fails and it appears likely that the unlawful discrimination will be repeated. Then the matter can be brought before the Courts, and if the Court thinks fit an injunction can be made by the Court requiring the offender not to repeat the unlawful conduct: if the conduct is repeated then this is a breach of the injunction and a contempt of the Court and is dealt with by the Court as such. Unlawful discrimination is a civil offence and not a criminal one, unless contempt of the court is involved. The Courts can award damages for loss of opportunity or for real expenses suffered as a result of unlawful discrimination.

Discrimination is only unlawful if it is on grounds of colour, race, ethnic or national origin. Discrimination on grounds of sex, religion, political belief or anything else is not unlawful.

There are many sections of the law that may be applied to immigrants, not as immigrants but as citizens: the provisions of the Infectious Diseases Regulations, Housing Acts, Public Health Acts etc. which may be of particular concern to the worker in this field will be dealt with in other chapters.

CHAPTER 5

THE IMMIGRANT AND THE PUBLIC HEALTH LAW

AN EXPANDING population has to live somewhere. Houses take time to be built and longer to plan and so the first result of an increase in the population is a shortage of housing. This causes prices to rise and the quality of housing available for a given sum to decrease. If the price of housing does not prove to be an effective population regulator—and it seldom does—then over-crowding will occur. The nature of the overcrowding will depend on the structure and customs of the immigrant population—immigrant that is in the sense both of newcomers to the area and of newcomers to the country. Of all the problems posed by immigration, housing is the most intractable and the most serious. The physical health of the immigrant can be assured without too much difficulty; the mental health is more difficult to achieve because our health services have until recent years been geared to physical rather than mental ill-health, but it is still a practical exercise. The achievement and maintenance of environmental health is of prime importance and is extremely difficult. Deficiencies in this field will rapidly affect the physical and mental health of the whole community and because the immigrant is more vulnerable in many ways the immigrant community will be affected to a greater extent.

Housing shortages and deficiencies have been the cause of a considerable amount of physical and mental ill-health in immigrant communities. They have given rise to resentment on the part of the indigenous population who are competing with the newly arrived immigrant from overseas for such housing as may be available: this resentment makes social integration and co-operation more difficult and this again breeds more resentment and aggravates the already difficult task of those who work within the social services.

The following notes on some of the problems which may be

57

encountered in the sphere of housing are therefore offered in the realization that many of the operative factors will be outside the control and even the influence of the field worker.

Overcrowding and Multiple Occupation

While it is unwise to make rigid generalization about the tendencies of communities to follow certain patterns of behaviour, nevertheless it is possible to distinguish differences in custom and attitude which can be useful in deciding what the main priorities are likely to be with regard to housing and the maintainance of health in an immigrant community. Housing accommodation may be obtained by rental or by purchase: in general West Indian communities tend to prefer to rent while Asian communities prefer to buy.

There is rarely an excess of accommodation available for rent and in areas where there is a shortage of housing it is almost impossible for the immigrant to rent a house. Because of the general preference of West Indian communities for rented accommodation, West Indian families will tend to occupy the only type of rentable accommodation available: the house let in multiple occupation. The Asian man will, if he is single or unaccompanied by his family, live together with his compatriots in a type of communal multiple occupancy or, if his family is with him, seek to buy a house. If he is unable to afford to buy with his own capital he will borrow from his countrymen and will lodge with them as the temporary tenant of an owner occupier until he has his own house. This type of multiple occupancy is different from that commonly found with the West Indian communities where it is much less common for the landlord to live on the premises and much of the rented property has been purchased as an investment and the landlord is remote—often so remote as to be traceable only with considerable difficulty.

When groups of immigrants first come to a town or city they very naturally seek out a compatriot for advice. Asians, in particular, tend to obtain accommodation from him or one of his associates. Before these groups increase in number and acquire more premises they tend to crowd into what is offered or available. Many must have come from inadequate accommodation in their own towns and villages and they are not appalled at living in circumstances here which most of the native population has long since rejected. Such overcrowding is very liable to increase the spread of infectious disease, particularly tuberculosis: it is necessary for the local health authority to ensure that the provisions of the 1957 Housing Act with regard to overcrowding are observed. Under the 1957 Act, overcrowding exists if any of the following conditions are fulfilled:

1. Two persons over ten years of age and of opposite sexes and not man and wife, sleep in the same room.

2. Where the room/person ratio exceeds:—
2 persons: 1 room
3   „   2 rooms
5   „   3   „
$7\frac{1}{2}$ „   4   „
10   „   5   „

In houses with more than five rooms, two persons are added for each room. All rooms, other than bathrooms and kitchens are counted.

3. Where the floor area/person ratio is less than:—
2 persons: 110 square feet
$1\frac{1}{2}$ „   90–110 square feet
1 person   70– 90   „   „
$\frac{1}{2}$ „   50– 70   „   „

These three conditions must be taken together in assessing the 'permitted number': the house is overcrowded if it is overcrowded under the terms of one condition only.

Infants under one year are ignored for the purposes of assessing overcrowding and a child between one and ten years is counted as half an adult. These are the legal limits and if the strict minimum requirement is observed the density of population is still too high by general health standards: such 'crowding' is not all that uncommon as may be gathered from a study of the 1961 census of England and Wales. Parliament has been somewhat dilatory in revising the standard of overcrowding.

Section 90 of the 1957 Housing Act enables action to be taken by the local authority with regard to houses let in multiple occupation. Multiple occupation may be defined as more than two separate tenancies in one dwelling (including the landlord if he 'lives in'). Where overcrowding has been established, the Local Authority may specify the number to be permitted to sleep in each named room, leaving one room at least for community life and eating. It is generally satisfactory in practice to stipulate not more than two persons per room however large this may be and to reduce this figure for rooms of an area of less than 110 square feet. A number of local authorities have, under enabling clauses in the 1957 Act, passed a local Act through Parliament to enable them to exert greater control over houses let in multiple occupation. Under such legislation it is usual to provide for the registration of all houses let in multiple occupation and for registration and prior approval of houses which it is proposed to let in multiple occupation. On registration, certain information has to be given, e.g.:—

(a) total number of rooms;

(b) number of kitchens, bathrooms and other rooms;

(c) total number of basins, sinks, fixed baths and showers and waterclosets;

(d) ownership and management details;

(e) number of persons, individuals and households, as the stated or proposed maximum number.

The local Act passed for Birmingham City Corporation laid down the following grounds for refusal:—

(a) house unsuitable and incapable of being made suitable for letting in multiple occupation at all, or as proposed;

(b) house in a locality the amenity or character of which would be injured by such a letting;

(c) the person having control or person intended to have control not a fit person so to do.

The Birmingham Act gives the right to appeal against the decision of the Local Authority to the County Court.

Such legislation enables a Local Authority to exert adequate control over houses let in multiple occupation and is almost a necessity in areas where multiple occupation exists on other than a small scale. Although the 1957 Housing Act enables action to be

taken if multiple occupation exists, a local Act such as described
above enables action to be taken before multiple occupancy occurs.
Prevention in such matters is often easier than cure.

It should be noted that adequate means of escape in case of fire
must be provided by the person having control of a dwelling let in
multiple occupation. The risk of fire in such a dwelling is high and
fires from inadequately protected heating appliances, particularly
paraffin heaters, are still common in spite of much publicity about
fire hazards. Regular visits to houses let in multiple occupation and
to other houses in which overcrowding is liable to occur is necessary as they enable an accurate check to be kept and, by 'showing
the flag', indicate that the Local Authority is serious in its inten-
tions. It is necessary only with persistent offenders to take legal
action.

Rented Houses

A rented house in a poor area of the town is often unfit in some
respects. Often tenants are unaware of their rights and may be
actively persuaded against insisting on their rights when they are
aware of them. There is a national shortage of Public Health
Inspectors and thus it is not possible to inspect all houses which
may be unfit at sufficiently frequent intervals. A great deal can be
done by voluntary agencies and by community leaders to remedy
abuses and to inform tenants and landlords of what is required
where ignorance of the desired standards is present. Some non-
profit making housing associations have been formed, often with
the active interest and aid of the local authority and these have
done much to improve standards of housing. Often landlords have
acquired property in order to make a quick profit and are unaware
of and uninterested in what is required to produce and maintain a fit
house. In addition such landlords may run their affairs in such
confusion and with a complete lack of business efficiency that in
spite of a large gross profit they get into debt and their creditors
are forced to take possession of a delapidated and decaying
property, sometimes with the expulsion of the tenants and the
worsening of the housing situation. With good business management a large number of houses can be let in multiple occupation at

a fair rent and maintained at a good standard to give accommodation for a number of years. (Ref. London Housing Trust, Lambeth).

House Purchase

As with any other community, the cheapest housing is the poorest in structure and locality. The first wave of immigrants acquire property in downtown situations and sometimes this property has been marked for slum clearance. Later arriving immigrants, even if they can afford the higher prices of houses on the outskirts do not seek accommodation there but prefer to live in and, later, to buy houses adjoining those already occupied by their compatriots. From their point of view this has a number of advantages, chief among which are that their wives can converse with neighbours in their own tongue and can obtain assistance with shopping in a new and strange place. In addition concentration of a population with the same customs makes worthwhile the opening of shops staffed by immigrants which sell the types of foods to which the community are accustomed.

Many of those buying houses will have had no experience of owning and occupying the type of houses that are constructed in this country and are unaware of the necessity of keeping the house in a fair state of repair. Small but basic items of repair tend to be left until the defect is a large one and therefore expensive to remedy. If the immigrant is purchasing his house by instalments he may not have the capital reserve to cope immediately with large repair bills and this position will be aggravated by the fact that local contractors may be reluctant to work for customers who do not speak much English and who may be thought not to have the means to settle an account promptly. Indeed some contractors may demand payment in advance before starting work and this can lead to a number of difficulties including further neglect of the now urgent repairs. One of the most common areas where repairs and maintainance are neglected is the drainage system and trouble with the sink waste pipes, rain water pipes and waterclosets may progress to a stage where the local authority takes action to abate a nuisance under the Public Health Act of 1936. Sometimes these troubles are reported by the immigrant occupiers to the Health

Authority as they believe that they will get the work done through the Health Department at a fair price. Notices to abate this type of nuisance are served fairly frequently as there will often be a considerable delay in effecting repairs without the stimulus of a notice. Notices may also have to be served to abate nuisances caused by dumping of rubbish and refuse in back yards by those who are unaware of the refuse collection services and the requirements of the Public Health Law on this subject.

This neglect of house maintainance is a partial one and is confined largely to certain aspects of the outside of the dwelling: rarely does action have to be taken with regard to the inside which is usually kept in a good state of comfort and repair.

Rental Purchase

A method of house purchase which avoids the necessity of obtaining a mortgage and enables a house to be purchased by fairly small payments over a considerable number of years is that known as 'rental purchase'. This is seen more frequently in the north and midlands of England and is largely confined to inexpensive houses. By this system the tenant or prospective tenant enters into an agreement whereby they pay a sum, generally on a weekly basis, for a number of years, after which the house is theirs. The number of years involved is generally small (around 3–7 years) and the amount is not a lot more than would be paid as rent.

A person entering into an agreement of this nature is considered to be in the same position with regard to the responsibility for the repair and maintainance of the property as one buying a house via a mortgage agreement and is classified as an owner-occupier. The law that applies to the maintainance of a property in good repair by the landlord and which can be invoked by the tenant to ensure that the house is a fit habitation does not apply to those who are owner-occupiers. If a mortgage is taken out then there is the safeguard for the purchaser that the company granting the mortgage will inspect the house to ensure that it is worth at least the amount of the mortgage and is likely to retain that minimum value. The danger of rental purchase is that the purchaser may be persuaded into the purchase of a property which is unfit or liable to become unfit and which will be difficult to maintain adequately and that, by ignorance or neglect, he will not take the necessary steps to ensure an adequate inspection of the property on his behalf before he signs the agreement.

Rental purchase has been in operation for many years and is not confined to the immigrant population. However, it may give rise to difficulty when an immigrant enters into this type of agreement as he may be unaware of the legal differences: it is possible, because of his lack of knowledge, for the immigrant to be over-persuaded by a zealous salesman.

Voluntary bodies and community associations can give much useful information to would-be purchasers and because of the specialized knowledge which the local health authority has with regard to housing law generally and to the particular position of housing in its own area, co-operation between local authority and voluntary and community organization can be extremely fruitful.

Slum Clearance

Because immigrant communities have frequently developed in down-town housing areas they are almost inevitably involved in slum clearance programmes. Although they do not often oppose such programmes at a public enquiry, there is often considerable resistance to the efforts of the housing authority to rehouse them and this resistance is most marked in the Asian Communities. Housing estates are often on the periphery of the city and a move to these areas involves a longer and more expensive journey to work—a complaint which is certainly not made solely by immigrants! Also, as the immigrant is often recently arrived he will resist dispersal to an extent which is governed by the closeness of his own community. In a community in which the activity of the woman, especially with regard to activities outside the home, is restricted there will be further resistance to dispersal and the breaking up of the local community. This lack of desire to disrupt the old community and to take part in a new one is not a particular feature of immigrants: the same understandable and justifiable reluctance has been seen in rehousing schemes in this country since the end of the second world war (e.g. in the East End of London).

Often families displaced from their own community will gradually return to find their own accommodation rather than take up offers of local authority rehousing.

If, after an area has been declared a clearance area, housing in that area is sold, the local authority is not liable to rehouse the new owner and, in addition, the new owner will be paid compensation which will be usually less than the amount which he, in his ignorance, has paid for the property. There is opportunity for sharp practice in the sale of property in an area earmarked for clearance to the unsuspecting newcomer who may be unaware of the law and be unable to understand notices and documents by virtue of his lack of the English language. A local authority can serve a most useful function in this respect by giving information on property to prospective buyers and, in co-operation with voluntary and community associations, publicise the fact that this information can be had for the asking.

Food Shops and Food Premises

The West Indian, because he is used to Western European and American customs buys much of his food at indigenous shops, although if his compatriots open shops, he will probably buy from them as well. His food is prepared in a like manner to the indigenous population although more of it is fried. The immigrant Asian is unused to European foods and will buy his food from Asian retailers as soon as these open shop. These shops, especially when they are first opened are often not up to the standards required by English law relating to food shops.

Asians are often involved in the running of catering establishments and generally Asian immigrants are more liable to 'eat out' than are West Indians. These eating houses are also a source of concern to the Food Inspectors of the local authority whose task it is to see that the law relating to these establishments and to food shops is observed.

Food Hygiene Regulations

The Food and Drugs Act of 1955 enables regulations to be made

E

concerning food hygiene and the Food Hygiene Regulations were made in 1960. These regulations lay down general requirements concerning food businesses which may not be carried on in insanitary premises or in any place in which food is exposed to infection. Equipment used in handling food must be clean and packaging of food is allowed only on food premises—that is premises which have to be passed fit for food handling. (Part 2 of the regulations) Part 3 relates to persons engaged in the handling of food and these food handlers must be clean of person and clothing. Food must be protected from any contamination by articles in which it may be carried and must, with the exception of uncooked vegetables, be wrapped in clean wrapping materials. Wounds must be protected by a waterproof dressing, smoking and spitting are prohibited and if any person becomes aware that he is suffering from a disease likely to cause food poisoning or to be transmitted by food or drink, he must immediately inform the owner of the premises who must notify this fact immediately to the Medical Officer of Health. (More usually, it is the Medical Officer of Health who informs the owner of the event and who lays down the preventive measures to be taken). Part 4 of the regulations relates to food premises. Sanitary conveniences must be clean and efficient and must not open into a room in which food is prepared. A water supply, both hot and cold, must be provided in adequate amounts with soap, nail brushes and towels for hand washing. There must be adequate first aid facilities and accommodation for personal clothing. Sinks and other facilities must be provided for the washing of food and, in the case of equipment, with adequate hot water and soap or detergents. Drying facilities must be adequate. Food rooms must be well lighted, adequately ventilated and not communicating with sleeping places. The walls and floors must be kept clean and in good order to prevent pest infestation and refuse must not be allowed to accumulate in rooms where food is handled. Unless intended for immediate human consumption meats which have already been cooked must not be kept at a temperature less than 145°F or more than 50°F. Part 5 of the regulations refers to food stalls and Part 6 to vehicles and receptacles used in the transport of meat—these must be clean and capable of being cleaned and offal must be kept in separate containers: persons carrying meat must wear clean clothing. Public Health Inspectors engaged in the inspection of food premises have to be especially diligent in ensuring that the Food Hygiene Regulations are observed. There is a considerable amount of work required in instructing immigrant food handlers in what the law requires and the language barrier does not make this task any easier. Enteric infections are more common in countries with a warmer climate but this is not really an essential feature of a warm climate; it is rather an indication of poor food handling and general sanitary standards and this basic lack of knowledge of the standards necessary for clean food handling as opposed to the strict legal requirement occupy a great deal of time in education and persuasion. It is usually unnecessary to use legal powers of enforcement, except on the persistant non-observer of the law.

The Food and Drugs Act

Under the Food and Drugs Act of 1955, a food must be of the 'nature, substance or quality' demanded by the purchaser (Section 2) and must be accurately labelled and advertised (Section 6): also food unfit for human consumption must not be sold, offered for sale, exposed for sale or processed in order to sell (Section 8). Many immigrants who open shops in this country will be unaware of the law regarding the food they sell and some imported foods, exotic to the eye of the food inspectorate, will not be of the quality desired. Labelling and advertisement material both on the label and associated with the food or drink may be extravagant, optimistic or completely misleading and may be printed in languages other than English. These, and the more familiar foods as well, must be sampled frequently and the labelling and advertisement material translated accurately, especially in the early days of the establishment of shops by the immigrant community. Immigrant shopkeepers are generally appreciative of advice when they realize that the Health Authority is serious in its intent and is applying the law without favour or discrimination. Prosecution of the shopkeeper is not often required but the back-street producer of foods, drinks and medicines which at best may be harmless but which are generally not of the 'nature, substance or quality', may need a great deal of attention, and a prosecution in this field may do a considerable amount of good.

It should be noted that the sections of the Act quoted above refer to drugs (that is medicines) as well as to food. The immigrant community is liable to be exploited by quack remedies, especially those labelled and advertised with this aim, and this exploitation is by no means solely operated by their compatriots.

Meat and Slaughter-houses

Many Asians observe the Islamic faith and as part of this observance will not eat meat unless it has been slaughtered according to the requirements of the Islamic tradition. English law requires that an animal intended for food shall be rendered unconscious before slaughter (often referred to as 'stunning') and this can be done either by the use of a captive bolt pistol which fires a metal rod into the fore-brain of the animal causing an immediate loss of consciousness or by an electrical discharge across the head which also causes immediate unconsciousness. The animal is then killed by bleeding which is necessary to prevent bacterial contamination of the meat from the blood stream. Exceptions to this law are granted to communities whose religious beliefs require other methods of slaughter: communities granted such exemption are the Jewish and Mohammedan ones whose beliefs do not permit preliminary stunning of the animal. The Jewish method of slaughter is to sever the main blood vessels of the neck by a single stroke and in this case consciousness is lost almost instantly because of immediate anaemia of the brain. Mohammedan ritual merely requires the severing of the blood vessels in the neck so that the animal bleeds to death: if this is done with one stroke, death of the animal is almost instantaneous, if it is not, the animal will die more slowly.

The law concerning slaughter-houses is that they should be clean, kept clean and of a suitable construction to enable this to be done. Animals must not be slaughtered if they are unfit and meat must be kept in hygienic conditions and at a suitable temperature to prevent bacterial growth. All meat slaughtered in this country must be inspected and prior notice of slaughter must be given to the local authority so that the meat may be inspected: the whole carcass must be inspected and may be condemned by the inspector either wholly or in part if it is considered unfit for human consumption.

Because of the strict requirements of the Food and Drugs Act (Part IV) and the regulations passed under the powers of that Act, it has become increasingly uneconomic for small slaughter-houses to operate. A number of local authorities provide large modern abattoirs catering for a large number of animals and providing good conditions for slaughtering and the cleaning, inspection and storage of the meat. These establishments rely on a smooth progression of carcasses and it is not possible to stop the system to slaughter animals by another method. Because Jewish communities are long established they have their own arrangements for slaughtering and transport of meat slaughtered therein to the Jewish community: Mohammedan butchers are not long established and have not yet achieved generally effective arrangements.

Until the establishment of Mohammedan butchers' shops in the Asian communities, many Asians had little meat apart from chickens. Because the larger abattoirs are often not available to the Mohammedan butcher, he must obtain his meat from slaughter-houses in which the Mohammedan method of slaughtering is observed and which may be a considerable distance away. Often these slaughter-houses are less satisfactory from the health aspect than the modern abattoir and the conditions in which the meat may be transported may also be unsatisfactory, this is often aggravated by the fact that each butcher requires only a relatively small amount of meat and the vehicle used is not constructed solely for the transport of meat.

It is necessary for the food inspector to devote a fair amount of attention to this matter and to inspect regularly shops selling meat and the arrangements for the transport of the meat.

The Shops Act

In an established immigrant community, especially one wishing to buy exotic foods and accustomed to shopkeeping, shops occupied by butchers, grocers, drapers, tailors, hairdressers, travel agents and even banks catering largely for the immigrant community will appear fairly soon. Many of these shops will, if they can avoid the eye of the Shops Act Inspector, trade on Sunday and will keep open for much more of the normal working day than the indigenous shops. This is in accordance with the custom of the immigrants in their native land and has a certain amount to be said in its favour provided that the working conditions of employees are satisfactory. It should be noted that the indigenous population have an increasing disregard for many of the provisions of the Shops Act and it may be that the law will be amended.

CHAPTER 6

THE MIGRANT AND MENTAL HEALTH

REPORTS from those working on migration and mental health suggest that migrants are more likely to be mentally ill than stable populations: this finding holds good for all migrant communities regardless of colour, although stresses associated with discrimination are very liable to increase the incidence of mental illness.

A change of home usually produces some degree of stress. The extent of this stress depends on several factors and the individual's response to it depends upon the quality of his personality. The degree of stress is decided mainly by environmental and emotional factors. A move which involves considerable alteration in the social and physical environment causes much more stress than one which only produces minimal alteration in the physical environment. Emotional factors are determined by the extent to which relationships have to be broken or suspended. An entire family experiences less stress than an isolated member of a family who moves out on his own.

It is important to consider the psychological problems of immigrants against this background. The stresses which they face are essentially normal healthy human reactions and are inevitable. Internal immigrants face identical stresses but in this situation they are accepted as normal and the individual soon settles down. Very severe stress reactions have been seen in people who have moved from one part of this country to another, or even from one part of a city to another and also in University students living away from home. Where there are no other obstacles to be overcome and the host community is sympathetic and tolerant, most people achieve satisfactory re-adjustment in six to twelve months. The majority of immigrants to this country not only experience considerable stress because of the many factors disrupted by their move, but often find that numerous obstacles (some real, some imaginary), are added to their burden. Their move involves

71

considerable upheaval both environmentally and emotionally but they find little support during their period of resettlement, particularly if they are 'foreign' or 'coloured'.

It is best to study this problem by considering adults and children separately:—

Adults. A large number of immigrants are men who are either single or temporarily separated from their wives. Their initial problems will depend upon language difficulties as well as their attitude to the host community. Pakistanis and Indians usually have to face language problems but their attitude to the host community is relatively neutral. They do not appear to have much desire to integrate and generally remain separate, tending to form communities of their own in which there is considerable amount of help and support. The incidence of mental illness in this group is no larger than one would expect to find among single or separated Englishmen. The types of illness that occur in adults seem to be of two main forms; firstly, an acute psychotic breakdown which may occur within the first few days of arrival in the country and which may in part be precipitated by massive stress produced by the sudden change, and secondly, a group of mental illnesses marked by the insidious development of paranoid delusions associated with depression. These delusions may involve members of their own community or white women with whom the patient has been associating. The delusions are often coloured by cultural attitudes, the patient believing that his food has been poisoned or that his sexual potency has been destroyed by some mysterious agency. Other hypochondriacal ideas are not uncommon and language problems not infrequently create considerable misunderstanding. I well remember one man who was actually admitted to a psychiatric hospital before it was discovered that his real complaint was severe toothache, for which there was ample organic basis!

The response to treatment in mentally ill patients is surprisingly good, particularly when one remembers that the patient has to be treated by English doctors and nurses in a ward consisting largely of English patients. So long as immigrant patients live in the community their friends and relatives will devote unlimited time and money to their care and it may be several weeks before they actually seek assistance from the Mental Health Service.

Married couples from India and Pakistan usually settle remarkable well and do not show much desire to integrate—it may be they are not given much opportunity to do so. Nevertheless they adjust to the situation, usually make friends with other married couples and may act as caretakers for single friends and relatives from their homeland. Some of the women respond to the liberalizing effect of western society and assume the way of life of their native sisters. A number, however, seem to prefer a sheltered existence, and some of these may develop neurotic illnesses with hysterical features. It does not appear that there is an exceptionally high incidence of mental illness among immigrants of coloured, races, but there probably is a vast amount of loneliness, insecurity, bitterness and anxiety which is not adequately met. Those patients who develop some form of mental illness often present additional problems which make both diagnosis and management extremely difficult.

Experience would suggest that there is a relatively high incidence of mental illness among immigrants from Eastern Europe. They seem to be more sensitive to their immigrant status and this may in part be due to the fact that they do not have the political attachments to this country which many other immigrants have. Very severe depressive illnesses and paranoid psychoses seem to be the commonest forms of mental disorder in this group. It is possible that they require much more help in adjusting to their situation than has been expected and if this is not available, the families withdraw into a monastic existence which even their own countrymen may find difficult to penetrate. In this situation the children, as well as the parents, suffer considerably. Efforts to rehabilitate such families into the community require considerable patience and tact as these families are very sensitive to any suggestion of charity.

West Indian immigrants are in many respects at an advantage because they are not so handicapped by language difficulties and are more familiar with English culture. They do, however, have a sub-culture of their own which may estrange them from those who are endeavouring to help them. Obeah still plays a considerable part in the cultural life of many West Indians (ref. *Personality and Conflict in Jamaica,* by Madelaine Kerr, page 111) and influences their attitude and thinking when under stress, thus making them appear primitive to the host community.

The West Indian immigrant inevitably brings with him the class and colour conflict with which he has grown up. At home various political and social developments have produced some measure of equilibrium in this conflict but the move to a country with a predominantly white population may exacerbate hidden fears and prejudices and produce either servile obsequious behaviour or aggressive behaviour with paranoid tendencies. These reactions may lead to considerable unhappiness in isolated individuals, but where large groups of immigrants settle in one area a strong community spirit seems to be formed, which is able to contain the feeling promoted by this conflict. It is however a precarious situation which could lead to serious difficulties if initial severe provocation from the white community occurred. Married West Indian immigrants integrate easily with the more liberally minded members of the host community and are able to come to terms with the insults that they may suffer from those who are rigid and bigotted. Occasionally some stable immigrant families are disrupted by the father's liaison with a white woman. According to Madelaine Kerr this may be in part an expression of the colour class conflict which may impel a man to establish a relationship with a white woman even though she is physically and intellectually inferior to his own wife. Such behaviour is not uncommon within all racial groups and may simply be a sign of human failing without any racial significance.

The West Indian immigrant resents being classified as an immigrant and likes to feel that he is able to take his place in the English community without being subject to special measures or classifications. They strongly resent the admission of their children to special schools for immigrants and it has to be admitted that in many cases there is no need for this.

Development of frank psychotic illness seems to occur in much the same frequency as is found in the host community. The symptoms are however coloured by cultural factors and as a result the whole symptom complex may seem exotic and bewildering. In some cases the effects of drugs such as cannabis may complicate the picture, while in other cases the patients genuine fear of the Obeah man may present a picture indistinguishable from psychosis.

Children. The problems faced by immigrant children are in many respects greater than those faced by the parents. The child is, on the one hand, influenced by the way in which his parents are reacting to their immigrant status and at the same time may find an entirely different state of affairs in their peer group. They may be well accepted and even popular and may find this difficult to relate to the situation of their family in the community. There is little doubt that immigrant children are initially subject to a considerable amount of teasing but this conforms with the general pattern of childish teasing and soon ceases when a child is accepted, re-appearing only during fights and squabbles. When teasing does persist, one generally finds that the immigrant child is deviant in some aspect of his behaviour, or that he is being teased by a small group of children who are themselves deviant. A situation arose in school with two coloured children of the same nationality, one bright and a good sportsman, the other dull and spiteful. The bright child was never teased whereas the other was always known as 'blacky'. It is probable that where the difficulties arise involving immigrant children, factors other than race are operating and it is important for these to be recognized and defined.

Most children are able to learn two languages without difficulty and within a year or two are able to speak English more fluently than their parents: this may lead to problems within the family group. Parents may feel inferior and the children may be embarrassed by their parent's poor English. Some immigrant children attending Child Guidance Clinics have expressed a wish that they were 'really' English. Subnormal children may find the intellectual burden of learning two languages a serious handicap, but I have never ceased to be amazed at the achievements of extremely dull children in this respect.

The West Indian child may, in addition to problems created by his visual distinctiveness, be affected by the multitude of adjustments which are necessary. Madelaine Kerr in her book has described the Jamaican practice of leaving the care of the children to the grandmother. We have often found that children arriving in this country to join their parents have not seen them for several years and may not in fact know their father at all. Many children are therefore transferred from a sunny, rural Jamaican village to essentially strange parents in a cold, dreary industrial town and it is not surprising that this produces behaviour disorders. Mrs Anneliese Walker at the International Congress of Mental Health in London, 1968, suggested that accommodation problems and deprivation in their home life were additional factors in the aetiology of the psychiatric disorder discovered in children. These factors no doubt are important, but it should be remembered that family disruption and child minding has formed an inherent part of the culture of working class West Indian families ever since the days of slavery. Furthermore services such as Child Guidance Clinics are virtually unknown in the West Indies and behaviour which normally would be dealt with by the family in Jamaica, leads to Child Guidance consultation in this country. In addition, the West Indian parent's desire to establish an 'English' culture may lead them to seek help more quickly in this country. Most stable working class West Indian families have ideas that are more English than the English and when they first move into an English community they fear that relatively trivial misdemeanours of their children may cause them to lose caste and be branded as primitive and uncivilized. This fear may lead the parents to adopt a rigid authoritarian role which precipitates rebellion and ultimately anti-social behaviour in their children. I have seen several Jamaican fathers whose authoritarian attitudes were reminiscent of Mr Barrett of Wimpole Street.

The basic problem of immigrants relates largely to the emotional responses experienced by all human beings who move their homes. The majority of immigrants are able to cope with this problem within their own kinship structure and do not wish or need any special consideration apart from common kindness and respect. Certain groups face particular problems which arise from ethnic cultural and language differences. The field worker will need some insight into these problems if he is to offer intelligent and helpful support to immigrant families.

CHAPTER 7

CHILDBIRTH, CHILD FEEDING AND FAMILY PLANNING

IN GENERAL, most immigrant women desire a hospital confinement rather than to be delivered at home. The underlying reasons for this are numerous but chiefly there is the general belief that a hospital delivery is safest for both mother and child. In addition home conditions are often not suitable for a home confinement.

In many areas of India and Pakistan the midwife is of a completely different status from the English midwife: the former undertakes not only the delivery of the child but also the household chores and the lack of this 'ancillary' service is seen as a further advantage of hospital confinement. West Indian women have a more happy-go-lucky approach to antenatal clinics, childbirth, etc. but generally they prefer a hospital confinement. Frequently housing conditions are such that a home confinement would be difficult purely on grounds of available space and the size of the rest of the family group. There is in any case a strong move in current obstetric practice towards hospital confinement for all expectant mothers, often in association with an early discharge system for those with suitable home conditions and in whom such early discharge is medically acceptable. Because of the shortage of 'delivery' beds in some areas a priority system operates and immigrant mothers often receive a priority grading because their home conditions are not suitable for domiciliary confinement.

The provision of ante-natal care to the extent usual in this country will be unfamiliar to many immigrants, but the benefits are obvious and very little difficulty should be experienced in getting immigrant women to attend these clinics. If difficulty is experienced, then the underlying fault is most likely to be found in the organization of the clinic rather than in the missing clientele. In general, little difficulty has been experienced in getting Asian women to book early and to attend ante-natal clinics regularly.

West Indian women are less satisfactory clinic attenders but this is not so much due to a lack of appreciation in the latter of the benefits of ante-natal care as to a more happy-go-lucky attitude to life. West Indian women also tend to work during pregnancy and this results in a later booking and poorer attendance in the same way that it does in English women who go out to work. The obstetric disadvantages of working until late in pregnancy are the same in any racial group and the apparent increase in dangers to both child and mother from this cause in West Indian communities are not due to racial differences but are the result of different social and economic customs: customs which may themselves be modified for better or for worse by the simple fact of migration to a different environment. The first West Indian immigrants included a comparatively high proportion of single women who had come to this country to work and this made adequate obstetric care more difficult. The position has been changing recently and as more West Indian wives and families join their menfolk already here the matter has become much less acute.

Difficulty is often experienced in the lack of a sense of 'timing' in the Asian women: timing in the sense of the duration of their pregnancy rather than the keeping of appointments. Quite a high proportion of them have little idea of when their last period was and it is difficult, therefore, to assess the duration of pregnancy from the date of the last menstrual period. This difficulty is experienced in the first pregnancy rather than later ones, possibly because constant questioning with regard to the date of the last period has made the mother realize that this information is anxiously sought after by the obstetric authorities. There may be considerable difficulty in the diagnosis of a post-maturity in an Asian woman unsure of the date of her last menstrual period, and this has caused one obstetrician at least to resolve never to diagnose post-maturity in an Asian woman.

The taking of blood for the routine blood tests may cause some anxiety, particularly with Asian women. This is generally not due to any superstition with regard to the blood itself, but a lack of appreciation as to how much blood the normal person has. Some women seeing five to ten mls. of blood drawn off in a syringe may feel that a considerable percentage of their blood has been lost, and the feeling of faintness and weakness resulting from this thought serves to confirm their first suspicions. A little gentle explanation by the person taking the blood or by the interpreter is usually sufficient. The expectation of feeling weak following the taking of a blood sample is not confined to immigrants but may present itself more frequently and with greater severity in them than in members of the host community, particularly during the first few attendances at the ante-natal clinic when the patient has not yet become resigned to the frequent taking of blood samples practised in our clinics.

Failure of the mother to notify the midwife in the early stages of labour may cause some concern. It has been noticed in some towns with a number of Asian immigrants that a considerable number of babies are born before the arrival of the midwife. There are a number of factors involved in this: the mother may not speak any English and be unable to communicate with the midwife: she may not know how to use a telephone and will remain sitting at home waiting the arrival of the men of the house who do understand how to make a telephone call. Some immigrant mothers, being unaccustomed to the provision of medical aid for the normal birth on the scale usual in this country, may not comprehend the differences in the routines surrounding birth here and in the countries from which they have come. This is more likely to cause difficulty where the immigrant community is small: where a larger and longer established immigrant community exists the woman is more likely to have friends and neighbours speaking her language who will be aware of her needs and whose aid can be summoned by a bang on the wall. Such difficulties are more apparent with recently arrived immigrants and with the first confinement in the host country. It must be realized that even in a town with a fairly large immigrant population there may be just as acute a lack of neighbourly help among immigrants as in English suburbia or in the early days of a new town. Just because 'they' may look all the same to some native eyes, it does not follow that a growing community of immigrants, who have probably come from a wide variety of backgrounds, can take up the closeness and good neighbourliness of an established village or district community any more quickly than could the indigenous population. With immigrants who do not speak the language of the host country the difficulty of communication from patient to midwife is obvious. What is sometimes not so obvious is the difficulty of communication between midwife and patient. There is always a tendency on the part of the medical staff to expect their patients to be aware of the normal routine with a minimum of information provided, forgetting that what is routine to the staff is a unique experience to the patient. If the patient does not understand English, considerable difficulty may result, but, by the use of an interpreter later difficulties can be avoided. If the patient understands a little English, the tendency is to expect them to understand more than they do and misunderstanding replaces incomprehension: the former can be more destructive of time and patient-staff confidence than the latter.

It is the responsibility of any medical or clerical staff to ensure that they understand what is said to them by their patients and that they in their turn are understood. If an interpreter is necessary, then one should be provided, but whenever possible a person speaking the language understood by the patient *and* qualified for the professional duties being undertaken should be used.

Special consideration may be necessary with Muslim women at the time of the fast of Ramadan. Difficulties may arise not only as a result of orthodox religious beliefs but also from different interpretations of the faith as practised by different communities, especially those without knowledge of modern clarifications of religious thought on the subject. The official viewpoint is that a pregnant woman need not, indeed should not fast, but many communities believe that their pregnancy will be more successful if they undergo fasting and a number of pregnant women do in fact observe the fast. Some may decline to take any medication by mouth during the hours of daylight and may even refuse injections. Difficulties will vary with the particular community from which the person has come and are experienced more often in those from rural areas than in those coming from the town. If it is necessary for a person to receive medication during the time of the fast and objection is raised to this, then the advice and help of the religious and social leaders of the community should be sought. Often women are more keen to fast in pregnancy as they are not able to fast during the time of menstruation: if they are not pregnant, the month's fasting will be interrupted whereas during pregnancy they are able to fast for a complete month.

In some communities, especially remote rural ones, a woman may not be willing to touch the placenta and the midwife would therefore have to deal with the matter completely. A midwife who was practising in a remote Asian community once arrived to find child, placenta and cord lying unattended in the bed next to the mother: this would be a very rare happening in any community and is now absorbed into teaching lore as an extreme example of a lack of awareness of the facts of childbirth.

In some remote rural communities a number of the women seem to lack knowledge about their natural functions and with this lack of knowledge goes the belief that it is not good for them to know about such things. Removal from a village community where such beliefs are held to a completely new environment should make health education on this matter easier, and there is considerable opportunity for advice and education from more knowledgeable women in the immigrant's own community. It is important that health education in an immigrant community should not only be directed towards the spread of enlightenment from outside, but that members of the community, having received this new knowledge, should in turn pass it on to other members of their own community. Because of the language barrier and the resulting staff shortage it is quite impossible for the midwife and health visitor to give *all* the information to *all* their patients, and a great deal can be done by encouraging informed discussion within the patients' own community. In the long run, this type of health education will be most successful, particularly in Asian communities where the women are more confined to the house than is the custom in other communities. Generalizations can be made only in broad terms and there will be considerable variation in knowledge, social custom and outlook within any community, indigenous or otherwise.

Infant Feeding and Weaning

Bottle feeding is accepted as a legitimate, even a desirable method, of infant feeding by immigrant women who in their indigenous

F

communities would not have considered any method other than breast feeding. In some respects this may be a conscious adoption of the ways of the host community where bottle feeding is practised by the majority of mothers. There is also, with some Asian women, the belief that because a number of accustomed foods are not readily available, the breast milk will not be of adequate quality and therefore artificial feeding is a necessity. Sometimes the baby may be bottle-fed and breast-fed, bottle feeding being seen as a supplement to what is believed to be an inadequate supply of natural milk. On the other hand in a few instances breast feeding is excessively prolonged: occasionally in the belief that breast feeding prevents conception.

In medical circles it is commonly recognized that gastro-enteritis is a particular hazard of bottle-fed infants. In a number of immigrant homes the general standard of hygiene may be poor, and, when this is combined with a lack of knowledge of the proper cleaning of feeding bottles, gastro-enteritis becomes an even greater danger. In most towns with a large immigrant population there is a significantly higher infant mortality among children born to immigrant parents and a considerable number of these deaths are due to gastro-enteritis. It is necessary for a great deal of care and instruction to be given by the health visitor in this type of household, and infants in this group must be considered to be at risk.

The feeding of small portions of adult foods to the weaned child is not in itself a cause of infective gastro-enteritis but may, by causing non-specific gastric and intestinal upsets, facilitate the advent of infective gastro-enteritis and render the clinical condition more severe. If the hygienic standard of food preparation is poor, then food with a degree of bacterial contamination insignificant to the adult digestion may be fed to a small child with disastrous results: this is often the basis of the gastro-enteritis associated with weaning. Generally speaking more difficulty is experienced in weaning the immigrant child than in getting the child on established milk feeds either by the bottle or by the breast. The weaning process and the advent of what one might describe as the 'junior dinner' stage is frequently associated with difficulty as the feeding customs familiar to the mother involve the substitution of milk feeds by a quasi adult diet. The intervening stages of cereals and junior dinners, which are almost invariably followed in weaning in this country is not the method that the women have been used to in their own communities, and a considerable amount of health education by the health visitor is required on this point. Again, the example and advice of members from the women's own community will be more highly regarded than advice given by the health visitor. A great deal of wisdom can be imparted at the ante-natal clinics by the mothers talking together and this state of affairs should be encouraged in all communities: in immigrant communities it is of even greater importance.

The proprietary tinned and packet foods commonly used in this country for the child who is being weaned are sterile and, although unfamiliar, should be strongly recommended. Generally speaking, standards of food hygiene are often poor and general cleanliness in the preparation of food lacking in some immigrant households. This is exacerbated by the fact that methods of cooking used in this country are unfamiliar and also that many of the foods themselves are unfamiliar. The results of not freshly preparing each meal are readily apparent in a tropical country as bacterial decomposition occurs rapidly. Many immigrant housewives believe that the weather conditions in this country permit them to cook food to last more than one meal or even more than one day without the aid of refrigeration or cool storage. Both the morbidity rate and the mortality rate from gastro-enteritis in immigrant children in many cities in the United Kingdom is several times higher than that in the indigenous community, and this stems largely from incorrect and unclean feeding. Failure to seek medical aid in time accounts for a much smaller proportion.

Some of the commercial tinned baby foods may be rejected on religious grounds although this is not very common. The manufacturers of baby foods have introduced some varieties to meet this objection: for example, the lamb and chicken dinners which are suitable for those who do not eat beef. It has been found that Hindu communities readily accept the infant dinners containing chicken but in some Muslim communities no dinner containing meat will be accepted: this is because of the belief that the animals used in the manufacture of these foods have not been slaughtered in the approved fashion. This problem may also be encountered with the adult and sometimes it is difficult to get the nursing or expectant mother to eat meat because of the belief that the animals are not slaughtered in the proper way. Frequently this belief is incorrect as in the modern abattoir the method of slaughtering is usually acceptable to the leaders of thought of the Muslim faith. However, information on this subject is not known by a number of Muslim immigrants or may be, in some cases, not accepted. Education in this matter lies in the hands of the leaders of the immigrant community: if there is any particular local difficulty, their advice and assistance should be sought. It is obviously bad practice to continue to recommend something which is completely unacceptable to a particular member of an immigrant community as this will tend to lead to an indiscriminate rejection of advice on all subjects. There are a number of very good vegetarian dinners for infant feeding and these are widely acceptable.

The use of the press, particularly the local newspaper, is of great benefit in health education, and should not be neglected with regard to matters concerning the immigrant community. Some local papers in areas where there is a large immigrant community devote a section of some issues of the paper to their needs and interests: when appropriate such sections are printed in a language other than English. The local press is a very good medium for health education and editors are generally willing to assist, providing that the health educator does not expect the entire paper to be devoted to the cause of health education! This method of contact is of particular use with regard to the newly arrived immigrant who has not yet known and become known to the community services. As the immigrant community becomes more established, the number of English-reading members rises and the advantages of material printed in the immigrant's own language diminish, although they remain of value in a limited number of spheres. As with health education anywhere, it is the person-to-person approach that is of prime importance, particularly within the immigrant community. Health education in an immigrant community is *in the essentials* no different from that in any other community, but there may be special problems of communication —and communication is always a two-way flow. As the first generation of children in the immigrant community grow up, the problems of health education become those of the host community and at this stage little differentiation of approach is necessary.

Generally speaking, attendance by immigrant mothers at infant welfare clinics is good and there are few problems of poor attendance.

The question of vitamin supplements may be important particularly in children with a darker skin. The amount of vitamin D taken in the food may be less in the immigrant child if there are difficulties in the family with regard to feeding. In addition the vitamin D synthesis will be less because of the screening effect of the melanin pigment in the skin. A number of mild cases of rickets have been seen due primarily to a lack of vitamin D in the diet but exacerbated by the lack of vitamin supplements. It may well be necessary for the health visitor to ensure that immigrant children receive some form of vitamin supplement particularly in poorer households where there is likely to be less than adequate diet. This difficulty may extend outside the age range normally covered by the health visitor: an inadequate diet may be received by children of school age, particularly where family beliefs do not permit them to receive school meals. In some cases where school meals have been refused it has become apparent that the child is receiving little or no food in the middle of the day, and the services of the school welfare officer may well be required in these cases. The problem again is not so much that this is a hazard peculiar to an immigrant household, but the fact that an immigrant is involved makes the problem rather more difficult to solve. There must be an especially good liaison between the various local government and other sectors of community and personal services where immigrant households are concerned as co-ordination of services is often more difficult on account of the language barrier. If it seems necessary, the health visitor should continue to visit households where a special risk exists after normal visiting and attendance at an infant welfare clinic has ceased. For example, the appearance of rickets in poor households has been noted recently: children from poor immigrant households should be regarded as a still higher risk for rickets as well as other vitamin deficiency diseases and kept under observation as a 'high risk' group.

One particular difficulty may be experienced with regard to vitamin supplements and other treatments in some Asian households: on occasions an over-permissive attitude obtains in the home and, if the child does not wish to receive any form of 'medicine' then the matter is not pressed: the situation can usually be resolved by some persuasion of both parent and child. It is well to remember that the child can receive too much vitamin supplement as well as too little. A case was recently seen where a small child was receiving Haliborange, cod liver oil, Adexolin and Delrosa, with the result that the child was suffering considerable discomfort from a rash caused by vitamin overdosage!

Family Planning

In most immigrant communities there is no religious objection to family planning. In the Asian households in particular it is important to approach family planning via the husband. Although the wife may have borne her husband several children, she may, in certain households, feel unable to speak to her husband about sex or family planning: frequent opposition to the idea of family planning is based on ignorance, and this ignorance is shared by both husband and wife. They may well be influenced by attitudes from the community in their country of origin: some immigrants may have been brought up in village communities in which the infant and child death rates were so high that a man would have to have at least two or three male children to make sure that he had a son to survive him: the historical necessity of large families would be of sufficient recent practical importance for the idea of planned or smaller families to be foreign in more senses than one. The attitude of the husband towards family planning may well be modified by the number of sons that he actually has. A father with four daughters and no sons might be less likely to consider family planning than a father with four sons and no daughters. Because of traditional beliefs, a male doctor would be considered unacceptable by some female Asian patients and a choice of male or female doctor should be available where there is an Asian community. Because many Asian women are dependant on their husbands for most decisions, the co-operation of the husband must be obtained by giving him any information he requires and by holding the clinic sessions at a time when he can attend. The mass approach is not indicated in this country, and all family planning from the initial approach through the giving of advice and information to the final application of the method chosen should be wholly personal.

The method of contraception used is considerably influenced by the person who is going to use it. If the idea of regular medication (the pill) can be got over, then this is probably the best method, but in many cases this is unlikely to be successful and mechanical methods such as the loop must be used. It may also be desirable to start contraception very soon after the birth of the last child: in a number of cases a single missed appointment has proved disastrous. In some cases the use of the pill diminishes the menstrual flow and, particularly with Asian women, this might be considered unfavourably as menstruation is regarded as a discharge of impurities. If, therefore, the flow is decreased, these impurities are thought to be retained and this can produce most alarming psychosomatic symptoms. The loop, on the other hand, may give a slightly increased menstrual flow and in these communities would be a point which would be considered in its favour. In a number of clinics the loop has been found to be much more satisfactory in the case of Asian women than the pill: other conventional methods are not particularly successful.

Some clinics have found that there is a significant failure rate with the intra-uterine device and this has resulted in the belief in a number of patients that the method does not work. There are side effects associated with 'the pill' which have reduced confidence in this method. Even the minor side-effects can become important as the reports of these can be passed from patient to interested friends and relations become much magnified and thus a potent factor against acceptance of family planning. Occasionally at family planning clinics too much information is given to the patient in the form of a long-winded weighing of the pros and cons and descriptions of the possible side effects: this is unhelpful and is to be deprecated as much as the giving of no information at all. After all, a patient expects her (or his) advisers in this and other fields to be expert and to advise them personally with regard to their individual needs: a simple, factual and brief explanation of the pros and cons is relevant but in the end the patient expects to hear 'this is the position, Mrs A., and in your case I advise method X'.

There has been in a number of cities much publicity given to family planning without much reference to the people who are expected to provide the skilled advice and technical knowledge. It must be realized that there is no method of contraception which is absolutely reliable and at the same time absolutely without side effects, and that family planning consists of rather more than contraception.

Well-meaning but ham-handed mass publicity is worse than none at all, as it will misinform and antagonize: probably the best person to raise the matter with the family concerned is the health visitor who, because she has some personal contact with the family, is likely to be viewed as a trusted and expert adviser.

Family planning advice is given to the unmarried as well as to the married by most family planning clinics, and often senior school groups may wish to have the facts of the matter presented to them. It is generally considered that adolescent girls and boys should be aware of the facts of life in respect of family planning as in other matters. Those who are concerned in giving guidance on this matter will be aware that the subject cannot be approached without consideration of the personal relationships involved: they should also take into consideration family tradition and custom.

CHAPTER 8

THE NUTRITION OF IMMIGRANT CHILDREN

THE MAJORITY of children arriving in England from overseas during the past decade have not shown signs of nutritional deficiency disease. That is not to say that they have been in an optimum nutritional state. The recognition of specific deficiency disease is relatively easy but it is notoriously difficult to assess general sub-nutrition. From the facts available it is reasonable to conclude that a considerable proportion of children, particularly those arriving from Asia have not had a good diet by European standards. The comments which follow are based largely on experience of children from Pakistan and the northern parts of India but they are also generally applicable to children from other under-developed parts of the world.

Most babies, especially those born in rural areas, are fed on human breast milk. Natural feeding by the mother is usually continued for much longer periods than the six months recommended in this country. In Pakistan and Northern India the average duration of breast feeding is only slightly less than two years, but in some individual cases may be as long as four years. The initial nourishment of these Asian babies is, therefore, ideal, not only because of its composition but also because the method of feeding affords some protection against common diarrhoeal diseases. Iron is the only significant deficiency in breast milk. Infants normally use iron stored in the liver in the later part of intra-uterine life to provide for their needs during the early months after delivery. The quantity of iron stored in infants depends upon the nutritional state of the mother and in areas of the world where iron deficiency is common, infants may not obtain adequate stores of iron before birth. This, together with the later age of introducing iron-rich foods into the diet, leads to levels of haemoglobin in the blood which are considerably less than normal. A comparison of the haemoglobin levels of Asian immigrant babies and English babies under one year showed an average difference of 16·9 per cent in haemoglobin. There was an increasing difference towards the end of the first year of life and fairly marked anaemia was not uncommon in the Asian baby.

The pattern of infant feeding by immigrant mothers after their arrival in England changes very quickly. A minority of their babies born in this country are fed by breast and artificial feeding with cows' milk is usual, despite its disadvantages. Early introduction of mixed feeding similar to the practice of English mothers occurs and, consequently, iron deficiency anaemia is infrequent in babies born in England to Asian mothers. The adoption of English infant feeding practices is not without hazard, particularly in the case of babies whose mothers are unable to read or understand instructions in English and who may be unfamiliar with the techniques of hygienic preparation of artificial feeds.

The nutrition of older children depends upon the quantity and quality of available food in the place where he lived. Average calorie supplies per caput in India and Pakistan fall short of the estimated requirements by approximately 240 calories per day. The available nutrients are not only insufficient in total but are also unequally distributed so that for some people in these countries, diet is considerably deficient in quantity and this may be aggravated at times by seasonal factors. Most children in Indian villages receive a diet having substantially less first-class protein than would be usual in England. Meat products are relatively expensive and there is a lack of modern cold storage facilities. As a result of this, meat is consumed only on an average of about two days per week. Other sources of first-class proteins such as eggs, milk and fish are available but generally in smaller quantities than would normally be taken in England. Diet in Asian village communities has a high proportion of carbohydrate foods and is often rather monotonous in character. The effect of the generally poor quality of diet may also be exaggerated by the prevalence of infectious and parasitic diseases which are a drain on the nutritional state. Children from Northern India and Pakistan are, on average, shorter in height and lighter in weight than children of the corresponding age in this country. The 50th percentile for Asian children corresponds to approximately the 25th percentile for European children, i.e. 75 per cent of European children are taller and heavier than the average Asian child. Inherited factors may be responsible for some of the difference in anthropometric measurements but it is probable that nutrition is a more important factor and there is evidence that children born in England to Asian immigrants are bigger than their brothers and sisters born in Asia.

Arrival in England has a number of nutritional advantages and disadvantages for the Asian child. The non-vegetarian child begins to consume an increasing quantity of first-class protein foods and, in particular, the number of days on which he consumes meat is doubled. In addition the quantity of other first-class protein foods obtained by him is also increased and, surprisingly, in many cases the quantity of vitamin C taken in the form of fruit is also increased. The vegetarian child may be at a considerable disadvantage because the variety of foods to which he was accustomed are not always available, particularly if he lives apart from the Indian communities in England. A further nutritional disadvantage which applies to almost all children following their arrival in England is the increased consumption of sweets. Dental health, good on arrival in the majority of children, quickly deteriorates and serious dental caries rapidly occurs in the months following entry.

Rickets, which is seen more frequently in immigrant children, particularly those in the pre-school years, than in English children, is a condition affecting the growth of bone and is usually due to a deficiency of vitamin D. The latter is available in fish liver oils, eggs and other dairy products, and may also be formed in the human skin by ultra-violet rays present in sunlight. It occurred more commonly in northern industrial communities because of the lack of sunshine and because of atmospheric pollution with smoke. In climates where skin is exposed to sunlight, less vitamin D is required in the diet but in this country it is necessary for infants to take a regular supplement of vitamin D in the form of cod liver oil, halibut liver oil or similar preparations with which Asian mothers are not familiar. Elimination of the disease will depend upon education of the parents in the need to supply vitamin preparations.

Vitamin C is necessary for the health of connective tissues and a diet deficient in it leads to the disease scurvy. The main sources of vitamin C are fresh fruit and vegetables and these are part of the normal diet in most of the Indian sub-continent. In village communities the supply of fruit is subject to seasonal variation but sufficient vitamin C can be stored in the liver to prevent deficiency disease and scurvy has not been noted in immigrant children arriving in England. The most vulnerable age group is infancy and in their native country, young children are probably protected by the vitamin C contained in breast milk. In this country it is advisable for a supplement to be given in the form of daily orange juice, rosehip syrup or blackcurrant juice.

Other vitamin deficiency diseases are similarly uncommon. Thiamine (vitamin B_1) deficiency, which causes beri-beri in some parts of the East, has not been seen in children from Northern India and Pakistan. In these areas the staple cereal is whole-wheat flour used to make chapattis and the wheat germ contains a quantity of vitamin B_1. Low levels of vitamin B_{12} are occasionally seen in children who take strictly vegetarian diets and this results in anaemia and neurological abnormalities.

Religious beliefs with regard to diet present a number of special problems. Children from strictly vegetarian families seem to be particularly likely to suffer from dietary deficiency. Education is required in the range of protein containing vegetables available in this country. Partial vegetarianism may also result from uncertainty about the method of slaughter of animals fulfilling various religious requirements and Mohammedan children often decline to eat the meat portion of school meals although they are not vegetarians. Pork flesh is taboo to Islamic children and strict Muslims require that cows or sheep consumed by them should be slaughtered by cutting the animals' throats. Hindu children, on the other hand, cannot eat beef and commonly assume that all meat presented to them in English schools is from the cow. These religious beliefs have to be respected but it is unfortunate that they concern the types of protein food which would often be of greatest benefit to the individual child. There is a case for providing an alternative and acceptable form of first-class protein food in school meals wherever this is practicable. Finally there is the question of religious fasts, the most notable being the Muslim fast of Ramadan. During the lunar month in which it is observed, Muslims take no food or drink between sunrise and sunset. From the point of view of the total nutrition of the child this is probably not of very great significance since he is provided with substantial meals before sunrise and after sunset and the fast is concluded by a feast in which food intake is usually increased. The fast applies only to children over the age of twelve years although some strict parents may wish it to be observed by children over nine years. Tiredness and lack of attention in lessons towards the end of the school day may result from the fast. Where this is very noticeable, teachers would be well advised to draw it to the attention of the parent and to ascertain his wishes in the matter.

CHAPTER 9

CHILDREN SEPARATED FROM
THEIR FAMILIES

THERE IS general agreement about the undesirability of young children being separated from their families, especially their mothers. It is emotionally damaging to many children and in some leads to emotional maldevelopment and diminished intellect. Immigration increases the possibilities of separation and it is reasonable to assume that in foreign surroundings the traumatic effect on children is increased. Careful use of the Social Services and strict observance of the law relating to child minding and child protection are, therefore, essential in the interest of the immigrant child.

The most common situation leading to the separation of young children from their parents is illness or confinement of the mother, requiring her hospitalization. Arrangements can often be made for older children to be cared for by friends after school hours until the father returns from work but in the absence of an extended family in this country it is often difficult to keep babies and toddlers in their own home surroundings. Where the parents are unable, because of disease, incapacity or other circumstances, to provide for a child's proper accommodation, maintenance and upbringing, and the Local Authority's intervention is necessary for the child's welfare, the Local Authority has the duty, imposed by the Children Act 1948, Section 1, of receiving the child into their care for as long as the welfare of the child appears to require it.

The Childrens' Officer may decide to place such children either in a foster home or in a residential children's home or nursery. In either event, two major problems frequently occur in immigrant children between the age of eighteen months and five years. Firstly, the child is suddenly unable to understand or to communicate in speech since many Asian pre-school children are brought up in non-English speaking homes. Secondly, there is often a

94

considerable change in the food received by the child. Unfortunately, the number of immigrant families able or willing to act as foster parents has so far been very limited and at present almost all children are looked after by English-speaking families. The abrupt change of environment, frequently unavoidable, often has a marked effect on young Asian children, a significant proportion appearing to be anxious and a few being depressed and anorexic. Any actions calculated to minimize cultural changes in care of the child are clearly desirable.

Some immigrant parents may wish to make private arrangements for their children to be looked after by a foster mother, for example where both parents are in employment or in receipt of full-time education. Others may wish to act as foster parents for financial reward. The Children's Act, 1958 provides for the protection of children living away from their parents and charges foster parents with specific duties. A foster child is defined as a child below the upper limit of the compulsory school age whose care and maintainance are undertaken for reward for a period exceeding one month by a person who is not a relative or guardian of his. Exemption is specified in the case of certain children in hospitals or placed in foster care by local authorities or voluntary organizations. Any person proposing to maintain as a foster child a child not already in his care must give written notice of his intention to the Local Authority not less than two weeks before he receives the child, unless in an emergency, when notice must be given within one week after receiving the child. Changes of address must be reported two weeks in advance, and if the foster child dies, is removed or removes himself, the Local Authority have to be informed within forty-eight hours. Default of these requirements may lead to fines or imprisonment on summary conviction. The Local Authority has the duty to arrange for each foster child in its area to be visited by an officer who must be satisfied as to the well-being of the children and must give any necessary advice as to their care and maintainance. He has authority to inspect premises and the Local Authority may impose requirements as to the conditions under which children may be kept. If they are of opinion that the circumstances would be detrimental to the child the Local Authority may prohibit a person from keeping foster children on those premises. In addition, certain unfit persons are disqualified from keeping foster children.

Newly-arrived immigrant parents may have difficulty in assessing the suitability of private foster homes into which they may wish to place their children. The law affords some protection provided that the foster home is registered with the Local Authority and, therefore, inspected by its staff. There is the possibility that foster care may be undertaken illegally by persons who have failed to notify the Local Authority of their intent, either because of disregard or ignorance of the law. It is important that immigrants proposing to act as private foster parents should understand the need to notify the Local Authority, the purpose of registration and that a reasonable high standard of facilities will be required before fostering arrangements are approved.

Similar protection is afforded to children looked after in private nurseries or by people minding children during the day, for reward. The Nurseries and Child Minders Regulation Act 1948 requires Local Health Authorities to keep a register of nurseries in their area and, in addition, of persons who, for reward, receive children under the age of five, into their homes. Any person wishing to open a day nursery or to undertake minding of children in their own homes must apply for registration and penalties may be incurred by default. Registration may be refused if the Local Health Authority is satisfied that any person employed is not a fit person to look after children or if the premises are not fit to be used for that purpose. The number of children to be received is specified and requirements may be imposed concerning the qualifications of the person in charge, the number and qualifications of the staff, the structure and equipment of the premises, and the arrangements for feeding, medical supervision and the maintenance of records.

The Nursery and Child Minders Act 1948 was amended by the Health Services and Public Health Act, 1968, Section 60. This more recent legislation states that registration is required for premises where children are received to be looked after for the day or an aggregate duration of two hours or longer for a period not exceeding six days. The original enactment did not require registration if the children received were relatives or if they did not exceed two in number or did not come from more than one household. This was amended and a person minding for reward, any child of whom he is not a relative now has to register. Local Health Authorities may refuse to register premises if they are satisfied that they are not fit to be used for child minding, because of the condition, equipment, situation, construction or size of the premises or for any reason in connection with other persons in them. In assessing the number of children that a child minder may be registered to receive Local Health Authorities must have regard to the number of any other children who may from time to time be in the house.

Requisite to the normal development of children is that they should have not only reasonable physical care, but also opportunities to learn through play and exploration. Lack of a reasonably stimulating environment and restriction to small confined rooms over long periods of early infancy may lead to educational subnormality when the child starts school. It is, therefore, of the greatest importance that they should have adequate play materials and the space and freedom in which to use them. In warm climates children probably obtain many formative experiences out of doors, to an extent that is not practicable in most English industrial cities. Some young children of immigrant mothers are at a disadvantage in this respect because of restricted accommodation or lack of appreciation by their parents of the need to play within the home, or possibly because of day minding in unsuitable premises. This is clearly a matter of fundamental importance to the individual child and it has far-reaching implications to society. Education of parents can do much to alleviate the problem but in addition, adequate play group and nursery class provision is essential as is the restriction of unsuitable child minding.

The families of a substantial number of immigrant children are divided, the father and some children, usually older sons, being in England and the mother and younger children remaining in Asia. Many of these boys live in unhappy circumstances and coupled with the emotional effects of separation from their families there is often a degree of physical deprivation. By comparison with boys living here in normal family units they are often in an inferior nutritional state, less clean and not so satisfactorily clothed. It is

G

usual for fathers to be at work for long hours and under these circumstances parental control and guidance must be presumed to suffer. There appear to be good grounds for restricting the entry to this country of children without their mothers but any future legislation which sought to restrict the reunification of families would prolong the hardship of children already here. There are, in fact, sound reasons for encouraging the immigration of mothers and younger siblings of these boys.

CHAPTER 10

THE IMMIGRANT CHILD AT SCHOOL

I T I S the intention in this chapter to note some of the factors which may make the reception of the immigrant child into the education system more difficult or less effective than for the average indigenous child. It would require a book to deal with all the factors and to detail the appropriate action. The field worker who is concerned about the health of an immigrant population will find that a considerable part of that population is of school age and therefore it is necessary to have some understanding of the particular problems which may appear in the school child.

Generally, immigrant children, whatever their ethnic origin, settle down happily in school. One of the best tests of the effectiveness of a school is whether the children and teachers are happy: fortunately most schools are effective when judged by this standard. There is no reason why immigrant children should remain classified as 'immigrant children': in most schools they become rapidly absorbed into the school culture and become simply children. The aim should be to achieve this state with the minimum of worry and fluster. The general rapid absorption and the happiness of the immigrant child in school is a tribute to the awareness of education authorities, the skill of the teachers and the adaptability of children.

Medical Examination at School Entry

Under the Education Act of 1944 provision is made for the medical examination of all children when they attend school for the first time. Because immigrant children will be coming to schools for the first time at all ages, it is convenient to make provision for the medical examination of immigrant children before school entry. Such examination is aimed at the diagnosis of any defects requiring special remedial treatment so that the child may gain the maximum benefit from school as soon as possible; to advise the parents with regard to such immunization procedures as may be necessary and to eliminate the risk of imported diseases interfering with the child's education. These aims are placed here in the order of their importance. It should be realized that school medical examinations are optional and that the parents may not wish for them to be arranged by the school authorities: they may in this case opt out.

Non-English Speaking Children

The inability to speak English should be regarded in the same light as an inability to see the blackboard or to hear the teacher: it should be diagnosed at the pre-school examination and interview and the degree of disability noted. Remedial action should be applied as appropriate. The facilities for teaching English as a second language and the method of dealing with the linguistically handicapped child vary considerably in England and Wales: where the numbers of such children are significant, then it seems that it is preferable to establish special centres, either for the children or for the equipping of teachers specially experienced in the necessary techniques. Inability to speak English adequately, inability to understand spoken English and also inability to speak English in an 'unbroken' form will give rise to teaching difficulties and to a failure to gain all that is possible from the education offered: this type of handicap will also act against immigrant children when they leave school and seek for work and will operate not only because inability to understand English would be a handicap in the work sought but also that inability to understand English is likely to be considered by the prospective employer as evidence of a less than adequate intelligence. It must therefore be the aim of the education services to remedy this defect as quickly as possible. There is almost as great a need in adult education in this field and where adult education is generally not well developed, much can be done through the immigrant community: it is fortunate that most non-English speaking immigrants have strong community ties.

Differences in Custom: Dress

It has already been noted that a number of customs may give rise to difficulties when the immigrant child attends school and these are seen mainly with the newly arrived child. The difficulties are generally not important and can usually be resolved satisfactorily: it is useful, of course, to have some idea of what customs are likely to cause difficulty and the basic attitude behind the custom.

The dress of the newly arrived immigrant child will often be that of the community from which he or she has just come: it is not desirable to establish rules regarding school dress especially in the period soon after arrival. The child will adapt quickly enough and the parents will usually be agreeable. It may be some comfort to the child to have some familiar things around while he is adapting to a strange world and adaptation is easier when not forced. Parents of all races are not very receptive to instruction from schools regarding their children's dress—or indeed in anything else—and this attitude is both understandable and reasonable. The *salvars* (long trousers worn by Asian girls) sometimes give rise to problems. Sometimes little is worn underneath and as they are often thin, they offer insufficient protection against the English climate. It is useful that parents should be advised about this, either by the head-teacher or by the health visitor. In established communities this advice will often be given to the new arrival by the community. Inadequate protection against the weather is not confined either to girls or to Asian children and attention should be paid to getting advice to parents when it is necessary. It is very rare that the parents are unresponsive or unappreciative; if they are it may be due to the way in which the advice is given rather than to the advice itself.

The *salvars* may also cause difficulty by the girl being unwilling to take them off for physical education or swimming classes: there may be variation between girls of the same nationality and also apparent lack of consistency in the same girl with regard to this matter. It should be remembered that the Asian girl is not accustomed to the uninhibited shedding of clothes that most indigenous school-children accept and may be acutely embarrassed by this. These matters are usually resolved fairly rapidly as the immigrant family settles into the new environment: making an issue of them is completely counter-productive.

Feeding

School meals may cause difficulty because the children may be completely unaccustomed to the type of food supplied. This is a difficulty not infrequently experienced in children taking meals at school for the first time, but in the immigrant child the difficulty is much more acute. Children are adaptable and they usually soon adapt their taste to that of their peers. It may be necessary to make it quite clear that no food which is prohibited because of the child's customs or religious beliefs, or those of his parents, is included in the school diet and some adjustment may be necessary to the menu for all or part of the children in respect of these foods.

School—Parent Contact

It is important that contact develops between the school head-teacher and the class teacher on the one hand and the parents on the other. To achieve this is often difficult whatever the ethnic group of parent or child, but may be more difficult in respect of the parents of an immigrant child. If the parents' command of English is poor, they may be embarrassed by contact with the school authorities and if one parent speaks no English the problem is even more acute. Many immigrants are not accustomed to being expected to take an active part in the education of their children and may consider that it is the job of the education authorities to fulfil this task unaided: they may also be used to a more authoritarian approach by all official bodies and the approach by the school may leave them a little non-plussed.

Dispersal of children has been recommended as a means of ensuring that schools consisting of a single racial group do not develop. This may be in some ways a desirable aim, but so also is the development of the community area school and the development of active parent-teacher contact. This can hardly occur if children live at a great distance from their school. Another defect of this system is that after-school activities are virtually barred to the immigrant child if he has to catch the school bus home immediately school ends. It may be that dispersal of children is not the solution and is being applied in an attempt to counter the adverse effects of non-dispersal of their parents.

Child-Care by Relatives

An uncommon but fruitful source of concern is the position when the parents return to their native country, or move to another town, leaving a child in the care of relatives. There are relatives and relatives, and care by a relative may be excellent or it may be non-existent. In some cases a child has been left in the care of relatives while he continues or completes his education and the standard of care has been poor: this may well occur if a boy has been left in the care of an uncle living in an all male household, where the members of the household are either sleeping or working and where the standard of nutrition may be inadequate, especially in the case of a child. The school welfare officer may need assistance from other local authority departments as well as from the immigrant community in dealing with problems of this nature.

The Stress of Adaptation

As had been mentioned in another chapter, the immigrant child is under a double strain: firstly, he has to adjust to a strange school environment and secondly his home environment may work against his adjustment in school. The background of many immigrant children may be a rural one and a number of those from Asia will have seen little of large towns or motor traffic. The sudden uprooting from a traditional rural environment to a British industrial town with its noise, its traffic and its buildings will leave the new arrival with a considerable sense of shock. This 'cultural shock' may last for days or even weeks and will be enhanced by differences in language and dress. In an acute form, it may present as a stunned silence in which the child may remain for several days. This type of shock may not be so obvious in the case of the West Indian children whose background may be more similar and for whom there is at least a basic common language. Problems arising from this source in West Indian children often appear later and persist for longer and are in part due to the continuing differences between home and school environment.

There are considerable differences in arrangements made for the receipt of immigrant schoolchildren whether or not they understand English. In some areas they are placed in a class with English children without special attention, in others they may be withdrawn from that class for special tuition and in some localities they will be received into a reception class in which they will receive intensive language and cultural tuition before they pass into the main educational system. Although this third method achieves less immediate integration the initial shock is considerably less, the security greater and the ultimate prospect far more hopeful. The rate at which an immigrant child settles in school will depend on many factors and will be influenced by individual variation. Girls tend to settle less quickly than boys. It is important to realize that in many Asian countries girls may be extemely conscious of the barrier between the sexes and it is thus advisable for them to sit with class-mates of their own sex, at least until they have settled in.

It is important that parents allow their children to settle in slowly and to realize that problems of adaptation among the children merely changing a school can be considerable: how much more, therefore, when they have not only changed school but a country, language and environment as well. The pupil-teacher relationship is, as always, of extreme importance. It is more important in the case of the immigrant child as the kindness and helpfulness with which he is met at school, which at that age is such an important part of his life, will influence his attitude and his attainments for the rest of his life.

Most immigrant children whether from Asia or the West Indies have been accustomed to a type of education which is, by present-day British standards, old-fashioned: relying heavily on learning by repetition and stern discipline enforced by physical sanctions. (This type of education is quite well documented in novels describing life in the latter part of the nineteenth and the beginning of the twentieth centuries in this country). There is little to awaken interest or stimulate the intellect and the child's main ambition is to keep out of trouble. In general, and it must be stressed that this is very much of a generalization, Asian parents, once they can be made to understand the educational system of this country, are anxious to encourage and help their children. Many West Indian parents, however, regard the permissive discipline and education by activity to be lacking in educational content and, in particular, in discipline. Most parents wish their children to get the maximum benefit from their education, but are troubled by differences between their child's new school and the system to which they were accustomed. This is particularly true in respect of the system of discipline: the discipline to which the parents were accustomed and by which they may rule their children is often harsh and unyielding and changes of mood are not easy to forecast. The resultant conflict between home and school discipline may result in considerable emotional difficulties in the children.

The freer form of discipline as practised in present-day schools in this country may, by its unfamiliarity, cause difficulty in adaptation in a child accustomed to a school with a more rigid type of rule. In this the conflict is expressed by the child over-responding to the freedom of expression in the classroom by being noisy or even unruly. This does not give rise to much difficulty unless there is a significant conflict between home and school.

Some children, and this is seen perhaps most frequently in West Indian girls subject to an overstrict home environment, are inclined to emotional outbursts of a type which would indicate a radically different problem if experienced in the indigenous child. After the outburst the child may attempt to resume activity as if nothing had occurred. This type of outburst may be a type of abreaction which is made easier by the fact that emotional outbursts of this nature are less unusual in the girl's own community.

In general, abnormal behaviour in school is rarely a manifestation of an evil intent in the child, but is a response to an impossible situation developing at home or between the home and the school. This response will show some differences in form in respect of immigrant children because their different cultural background will modify the way in which the response appears and may also make them more liable to particular kinds of stress. The basic response is one of distress and with understanding and experience of the different ways in which it can appear, may be appreciated and an attempt made to remedy the situation.

The reader is referred to *Children in Distress* by Clegg and Megson for a more detailed description of this phenomenon.

Child Minding

The problem of child minding in unsuitable surroundings by unsuitable persons has been dealt with in another chapter. It should be recalled at this point that inadequate child minding and inadequate parental attention may lead to poor intellectual development of a child by a failure to stimulate it. This can produce a child who may be completely unable to cope with school entry at the age of five years and in extreme cases could produce a child with a near autistic type of non-response.

CHAPTER 11

THE IMMIGRANT AND INFECTIOUS DISEASES

THE IMMIGRANT may be associated with infectious diseases to a greater extent than the average member of the indigenous population for two reasons: firstly he may, because he is a traveller, be involved in the importation of an infectious disease from the country of his origin to the country of his destination and secondly, because of his lack of specific resistance to certain infectious diseases he may be more liable to contract these after his arrival in the host country. Internationally the most important infectious diseases are the 'big five', namely cholera, relapsing fever, smallpox, plague and typhus. The most important of the infectious diseases in U.K. and Western Europe to which the immigrant is more susceptible than the host population is tuberculosis: this disease is dealt with separately in Chapter 14. The immigrant is particularly liable to upper respiratory tract infections soon after arrival; these infections are viral in origin. The common infectious fevers involve immigrant children to the same extent as the indigenous ones but, if there is an underlying malnutrition, the clinical severity may be greater.

The Health Services and Public Health Act of 1968 and the Infectious Diseases Regulations also of 1968 have introduced some important changes in the law concerning infectious disease. Section 47 of the Health Services and Public Health Act 1968 (henceforth abbreviated to the Public Health Act 1968) redefines the term 'notifiable disease': under this section a 'notifiable disease' now means any of the 'big five', that is cholera, plague, relapsing fever, smallpox and typhus. Section 48 of the Act lays down that if a qualified medical practitioner becomes aware or suspects that a patient within the area of a Local Authority is suffering from a notifiable disease or from food poisoning, he shall, unless he has reasonable ground to believe that the case has already been notified, notify to the Medical Officer of Health of that Local Authority certain facts. Notification is usually by post on a form which is provided by the Local Authority but would, in the case of a serious infectious disease, be made by telephone. The information required in the notification is:

1. The name, age and sex of the person who is thought to be suffering from the disease and the address of the premises where the patient is.

2. The disease.

3. Date of onset of the condition.

4. If the premises where the patient is are a hospital, the address from which the patient was admitted and the date of his admission.

The medical practitioner issuing the certificate is also required to certify whether or not, in his opinion, the disease was contracted in hospital. A medical practitioner in a hospital must notify all notifiable diseases and food poisoning to the Medical Officer of Health of the area in which the hospital is, regardless of the area from which the patient was admitted. The Medical Officer of Health of the area in which the hospital lies is responsible for re-notifying any case of a notifiable disease or food poisoning to the Medical Officer of Health of the area from which the patient came. This is a change from the previous law on notification. The doctor who is responsible for making the notification is the doctor in whose care the patient is. Section 52 of the Public Health Act 1968 enables a local authority to extend the categories of notifiable disease within its own boundaries. That is to say, a local authority can, with the approval of the Ministry of Health, make legislation to make any disease notifiable but naturally this provision is confined to the area of jurisdiction of the particular local authority.

Section 56 of the same Act authorizes the Minister of Health to make regulations relating to additional notifiable diseases: the Infectious Diseases Regulations 1968 which came into effect on 1st October 1968 were made by virtue of this section. Under these regulations the following diseases cease to be notifiable:

> Acute influenzal pneumonia
> Acute primary pneumonia
> Acute rheumatism

Erysipelas
Membranous croup
Puerperal pyrexia

Whereas tetanus and yellow fever are added.

The addition of yellow fever does not imply that the Minister believes that an epidemic of this disease is imminent; it is added because it is one of the international quarantinable diseases, and thus the law in the country is brought into line with international law on infectious disease.

The 1968 Public Health Act, therefore, makes the following classes of disease notifiable.

    (a) The big five.
    (b) Food poisoning.
    (c) Diseases added by the Minister.
    (d) Diseases added by a local authority.

Groups (a), (b) and (c) are applicable nationally, group (d) is applicable locally. Diseases in groups (a), (b) and (c) are as follows:

Acute encephalitis
Acute meningitis
Acute poliomyelitis
Anthrax
Cholera
Diphtheria
Dysentery (amoebic or bacillary)
Infective jaundice
Leprosy
Leptospirosis
Malaria
Measles
Ophthalmia neonatorum
Paratyphoid fever
Plague
Relapsing Fever
Scarlet Fever
Smallpox
Tetanus

Tuberculosis
Typhoid Fever
Typhus
Whooping Cough
Yellow Fever

Quarantinable disease are the big five plus yellow fever. Under the International Sanitary Regulations, the Health Authorities of a country conforming to the regulations are required to notify the existance within their jurisdiction of any quarantinable diseases to the World Health Organization and to take necessary measures against the spread of such diseases. These necessary measures are usually confinement and isolation of a case, surveillance of contacts and specific immunization if applicable: certain measures are taken against possibly contaminated articles or ships, and in the case of yellow fever, typhus and relapsing fever, specific anti-insect measures directed against the insect vector concerned. Persons arriving from endemic or epidemic areas without valid documentary proof of immunization against cholera, yellow fever or smallpox may be placed under surveillance for an appropriate period as if they were known contacts. Some countries have not signed the International Sanitary Regulations and thus are not bound by their provisions: in these countries precautions against imported infectious diseases are generally more stringent than required by the regulations: for example, a person arriving without a valid smallpox vaccination certificate might be put in quarantine rather than under surveillance.

A Medical Office of Health receiving notification of a quarantinable disease, leprosy, or malaria contracted in this country must immediately notify the disease to the Chief Medical Officer, Ministry of Health. Other notifiable diseases are notified weekly by the Medical Officer of Health to the Registrar General who publishes a weekly record of notifiable diseases, and some other vital statistics, in a weekly return which shows the total weekly notifications received in respect of each notifiable disease for the country as a whole, the main county and city areas and of each health authority area.

Food poisoning is notifiable under Section 48 of the 1968 Public

Health Act and is dealt with as a separate entity from notifiable diseases: the phrase constantly recurring in the legislation is 'notifiable disease or food poisoning'. Food poisoning refers to typhoid, paratyphoid and other salmonella infections, amoebic and bacillary dysentery and staphylococcal infections likely to cause food poisoning.

Typhoid and paratyphoid are considerably more common in a number of countries than they are in this country, and, because a person may arrive in the incubation stage of the disease or (particularly in the case of typhoid) may be a carrier, immigrants may be involved in these infections more than the average member of the indigenous community: it should be remembered, however, that holiday makers returning from holidays overseas or even 'holidays at home' are often involved in the importation of this group of diseases. Under the Infectious Diseases Regulations 1968, if a person is suffering from food poisoning or is believed to be suffering from food poisoning, or is suffering from or is believed to be a carrier of one of the diseases listed in the definition of food poisoning above and it is considered to be desirable for measures to be taken to prevent the spread of infection, that person may be required to discontinue or to refrain from engaging in any occupation connected with food until further notice: also other measures as specified may be taken 'for the protection of the public health to prevent the spread of infection'. The assistance of any other person may also be required, e.g. the manager of food premises, with regard to the employment of any person or with regard to facilities for medical examinations. Such requirements are made by the Local Authority acting on the advice of the Medical Officer of Health: in most Local Authorities the Medical Officer of Health is empowered by the local Authority to take action under this section of the Infectious Diseases Regulations on their behalf, informing them of the matter as soon as is reasonable. Compensation is paid by a local authority to any person who ceases his or her employment on the direction or request of the local authority to prevent the spread of disease. In all but a very few cases a request of this nature and requests for medical examination (which is usually in fact a bacteriological examination of a faecal specimen) meets with helpful co-operation from the person concerned: Section 54 of the

1968 Public Health Act gives power to a Justice of the Peace to order the medical examination of a group of persons believed to include the carrier of a notifiable disease. This represents a strengthening of the law as previously power was given only in respect of a person who was suffering from a notifiable disease.

Compulsory powers are rarely invoked, but they are available if necessary. Often misunderstandings occur between the Local Authority and patient and the barrier of language is a particularly fruitful source of misunderstanding as are explanations by those who are tactless, unsympathetic or merely overworked. It is important that the co-operation of all involved in the control of infectious disease be obtained and maintained: antagonized or ruffled customers will constitute a bad advertisement for the department and a sourse of difficulty in the future, as well as being generally unnecessary.

Schedule 2 of The Infectious Diseases Regulations of 1968 contains a most useful summary of the public health ennactments applicable to various infectious diseases and any who are involved in work in infectious disease control are strongly recommended to have a copy of these regulations.

CHAPTER 12

QUARANTINABLE DISEASES

THE quarantinable diseases are plague, cholera, yellow fever, typhus, relapsing fever (louse borne) and smallpox. Special provisions relate to each of them. The only one of these likely to involve the medical auxiliary is smallpox. A person arriving from an infected area, that is either an endemic area or an area in which the disease has recently been epidemic and which has not yet been declared free from infection, may be required to possess a valid international certificate of vaccination against smallpox or may, if he does not hold such a certificate be vaccinated and placed under surveillance: if vaccination is refused the person may be isolated for fourteen days. If an aircraft or ship arrives with a case of small-pox on board then that aircraft or ship is 'an infected vessel' and on its arrival the Port Health Authority may offer vaccination to any person insufficiently protected, isolate or place under surveil-lance any person disembarking up to fourteen days after their last exposure to infection and also disinfect the baggage or bedding of any infected person.

In the case of an aircraft, the fact that it was an 'infected vessel' is often not discovered until after the passengers have left for their various destinations. In the United Kingdom no record of passengers, their destinations and their ports of origin is kept and this occasionally makes life of a would-be controller of infectious diseases more arduous than would appear to be necessary.

International Certifications of Immunization

The International Sanitary Regulations enable a Health Authority to require certificates of vaccination against cholera, smallpox and yellow fever from travellers entering the territory of that Health Authority. These requirements relate not only to the country of origin of the traveller, but also to the countries in which the traveller disembarks during his journey, unless he remains in the direct transit area of an airport. The airport in question would be kept free from international quarantinable diseases by the country administering it.

Certificates of vaccination against three diseases only may be required: namely, cholera, smallpox and yellow fever. These certificates are required from travellers coming from a country or travelling through a country in which these three diseases are endemic or in which they may be existing in epidemic form at the time of the journey.

A book is published by the World Health Organization listing the vaccination certificate requirements for international travel according to the country of destination. The World Health Organization maintains the accuracy of this publication by the periodic publication of amendments. The requirements regarding vaccination against the three diseases are listed and the conditions required for each given. In order to be able to advise the traveller effectively with regard to his international obligations concerning the vaccinations required by the country of destination, an up-to-date publication on vaccination certificate requirements should be consulted.

There are certain exemptions from vaccinations: most countries do not require vaccination certificates in the case of infants and the age at which immunization is a requirement is stated in the World Health Organization publication. There is also an exemption given if the vaccinator is of the opinion that vaccination is contra-indicated on medical grounds; the most common example of this is in the case of vaccination against smallpox. A person, for example someone suffering from severe eczema, in whom vaccination against smallpox is considered to be medically contra-indicated should be provided with a certificate from the medical practitioner making this decision, stating in writing the reasons underlying his opinion. A certificate from the local Health Authority of the person's country of origin should also be provided stating that the Health Authority Area is free from smallpox and this certificate is issued as near as possible to the date of the person's journey. Most Health Authorities will accept these two certificates but there is no binding agreement in the International Sanitary Regulations that they will do so. In addition, certain countries, for example Australia, are not signatories of the International Sanitary Regulations and may not accept such certificates. In this case such persons could, if they could not be vaccinated, be required to undergo a period of quarantine appropriate to the circumstances of their journey. In addition a country that has not ratified its agreement to the International Sanitary Regulations may require immunization against other diseases or may require immunization against these three diseases under circumstances more stringent than required under the International Regulations.

Details about the method of immunization are briefly as follows:

Cholera. It is left to each Health Authority to decide whether one or two injections of cholera vaccine should be given; this decision rests with the Health Authority issuing the certificate and no country may require a certificate showing two injections. Generally speaking, however, two injections are given as an initial immunization and one injection is considered to be adequate as a booster dose. Immunization against *yellow fever* uses a modified live virus and must be given in a centre internationally authorized and recognized for immunization with this vaccine. Vaccination against *smallpox* may be done either by multiple pressure or a scratch technique. Most authorities would consider that the multiple pressure technique is the best (reference Ministry of Health Memorandum on Vaccination against Smallpox.)

Period of Validity of International Certificates

Cholera certificates are valid for a period of six months starting six days after one injection of vaccine. A booster dose given before the end of this period of six months renders the certificate valid for a further period of six months. The period of validity of International Certificates of Vaccination against *yellow fever* is ten years beginning ten days after the first vaccination or the date of a revaccination if this falls within ten years of the previous immunization. Vaccination certificates against *smallpox* are valid for a period of three years starting eight days after the date on which a successful primary vaccination was performed. In the case of a revaccination against smallpox the validity period of three years starts on the day of the revaccination. If an International Certificate of vaccination is deficient in any respect, it is considered not valid; a person who does not hold a valid certificate is considered to be in precisely the same state as a person holding no certificate at all. The action taken in the case of a traveller not holding a valid certificate or not holding any certificate at all is at the discretion of the Health Authority of the country in which the person is landing, but in the case of countries which are signatories of the International Sanitary Regulations, travellers will generally be put under surveillance for the duration of the period in question: only if they showed signs of a quarantinable disease would they be isolated.

An international certificate of vaccination or immunization must, to be valid, be printed in English and French and be completed in English or French: a third language may be added and the certificate may be completed in this language in addition to being completed in English or French. A valid international certificate must state the name, sex and date of birth of the person immunized and must also be signed by him—unless he is too young to sign. The date must be written clearly and not in a manner which might be misinterpreted. In the case of a vaccination against smallpox, the correct column must be used showing whether the vaccination is a primary one or is a revaccination and in the case of a primary vaccination the result must be read and certified as successful although it is not necessary that the person who does this be the person who performed the original vaccination. Since 1967 the origin and the batch number of the smallpox vaccine used must be recorded and the omission of this information leads to the rejection of a vaccination certificate.

The medical practitioner performing the vaccination or immunization must sign the certificate and give his or her professional status: rubber stamp signatures are not valid. The certificate must also bear the approved stamp of the Health Authority of the locality in which the certificate was issued. Generally speaking, if the vaccination was done by the staff of the Health Authority then the 'Approved Stamp' will state 'X Health Department': if the vaccination has been done by a family doctor then the 'Approved Stamp' of the Health Authority usually takes the form of a validation of the signature of the doctor performing the vaccination. An example of a correctly complete certificate is shown in Fig. 3.

Generally speaking it is the responsibility of the travel agency responsible for booking the person on his or her journey to provide approved forms for certificates of vaccination or immunization. These forms are sometimes poorly printed and errors in the wording in some essential part may lead to their not being considered valid at the port of entry. International certification is concerned with the risk of imported disease in the country that the traveller is entering: it is not concerned with the protection of the individual for his own sake.

Surveillance

In countries where smallpox is not endemic concern often arises when a person enters the country without a valid certificate of vaccination against the disease: if the certificate is not valid, then the traveller is considered to be in the unvaccinated state whatever other documentary or bodily evidence there may be to dispute this. For example, the batch number of the vaccine may be omitted: the person completing the certificate may have entered details in the wrong column or against the wrong line of the international certificate. If the certificate is not valid or no certificate is held, the incoming traveller is usually vaccinated or re-vaccinated at the port of entry and notification is sent to the Health Authority of the area to which the person is travelling requesting that surveillance measures be undertaken.

Vaccination offers a very high protection against developing the disease and the small minority who do develop smallpox and who have apparently had a successful recent vaccination usually develop the disease in a very mild state; this mild state may be so mild or untypical as to be unrecognized as smallpox. It is possible therefore for a person to enter the country apparently with a valid international vaccination certificate and yet either have smallpox or be incubating the disease. Therefore, if one wishes to provide 'absolute' protection against the introduction of smallpox in a country, short of prohibiting all ingress into the country, all persons coming from an area in which the disease might have been contracted should be placed under surveillance. The risk of such travellers bringing smallpox into the country while being in a vaccinated state is exceptionally remote and it would be quite impossible to arrange for the surveillance of such a large number of people, especially as it would include large numbers of highly mobile business men: it is adequate to provide surveillance for the unvaccinated only. The following scheme gives a satisfactory degree of protection to the static community against importation of smallpox.

On receipt of the notification of the arrival of an unvaccinated person, or a person not in possession of a valid international certificate from a smallpox endemic area, all such persons should be visited at the earliest opportunity. A note is taken of whether they are in possession of documentary evidence of previous vaccination against smallpox, the presence of scars of previous vaccinations would be looked for and a note made of these, and also of the state of the revaccination or primary vaccination done at the port of entry. In the case of a person with scars of previous vaccinations against smallpox and a successful revaccination performed at the port of entry, no further visits need be made if the Health Authority is satisfied that the person will notify the Health Authority if he falls ill within three weeks of his arrival. In the case of a person receiving a primary vaccination at the port of entry, daily surveillance should be made up to sixteen days after arrival. If the primary vaccination done at the port of entry is unsuccessful, the person should be revaccinated but surveillance need not continue longer than sixteen days after entry. A person with evidence of scars of previous vaccinations but with an unsuccessful revaccination done at the port of entry should be revaccinated and put under daily surveillance up to sixteen days after entry. 'Entry' and 'arrival' refer to the date of entry into the country from the endemic area, not to the date of the arrival in the local authority. If the traveller has not come directly from the smallpox endemic or epidemic area or has come by sea, then the times for surveillance will be modified according to the date the traveller had left the area in which he may have contacted the disease.

No restrictions need be placed on the movement of any person under surveillance who should be visited daily and have his temperature taken. If the person remains well and the temperature normal, no special report should be made, but, if either the person feels unwell or the temperature becomes raised, then the Medical Officer of Health or the appropriate Medical Officer should be informed at once. A person under surveillance feeling unwell or with a raised temperature would either be admitted to an isolation hospital or be put on more frequent surveillance, depending on the result of clinical assessment by the examining Medical Officer.

It is important that any person who may be suffering from or be in the early stages of smallpox infection be seen by a doctor who has personal experience of smallpox. The Ministry of Health publishes a list of smallpox consultants who are available to see and assess cases in whom there is doubt about the diagnosis. In general, the following basic assumption is advisable: any person developing symptoms which might be due to smallpox and who has been either a contact of a person suffering from smallpox or in an area in which he could have contracted smallpox, should be considered to be suffering from smallpox until proved otherwise.

Any person who is a contact of a case of smallpox should be placed on surveillance for a period of twenty-one days from the last date of contact: between the period covered by ten days from the first day of contact to fifteen days after the last day of contact with the case, the surveillance should be twice daily. The person should also be requested to report if he feels unwell. It is not unusual for a person being visited twice a day for smallpox surveillance to feel a little unwell: all symptoms, however, should be taken seriously.

The principle of surveillance is essentially constant but the details are modified with respect to the particular disease, its incubation period, its mode of transmission, its importance and its symptomatology. If the disease is not considered to be important, then no surveillance measures are undertaken. If it is considered of sufficient importance, then the important date to establish at the outset is the date on which, or the period over which, infection could have occurred and the nature of the infections: from these and a knowledge of the range of the incubation period applicable, the period within which the disease is likely to appear can be calculated. Surveillance is concentrated within this period and is applied according to the symptomatology of the disease: laboratory tests will be done, if they are considered relevant, but will be confined to the times at which they are likely to be productive. The establishment of disease will involve removal of the patient to hospital: the indication that relevant symptoms may be developing will involve isolation and observation at home or in hospital according to the individual circumstances—a decision which will be taken by the physician in charge of the case and to whom all untoward signs and symptoms developing during surveillance should be immediately reported. If the disease develops in a person under surveillance, then the contacts of that patient will be placed under surveillance as appropriate: 'contact' is used in the sense of a person to whom the disease could have been transmitted and the period of infectivity is important in coming to a decision on this point.

The vaccination or immunization of contacts and other persons under surveillance should be done if there is an appropriate and effective immunizing agent: this is a measure of personal protection for the individual and also for the prevention of spread of the disease but it is no substitute for adequate surveillance. In the case of a disease like smallpox, vaccination should be at least one stage ahead of the developing disease, taking the theoretical possibilities at their worst: for example, all contacts of a contact 'A' should be vaccinated before 'A' could develop the disease so as to become infectious, and if possible to give rise to immunity in the contacts before 'A' could infect them. If 'A' is a known contact but is protected by vaccination then he should be confined to his house in as small a circle of family as possible during the period in which he could develop the disease: if he were unprotected at the time of his exposure, then voluntary isolation in a suitable hospital would be indicated.

The following terms are used with regard to quarantinable disease:

Infected area: one in which a quarantinable disease is present, either in epidemic or endemic form.

Infected person: a person infected with a quarantinable disease.

Infected vessel: a ship or aircraft in which a person with a quarantinable disease is travelling or in which such a person has travelled within a stated period.

Suspect: a person who is not diagnosed as an infected person but who may have been infected and could therefore be capable of transmitting the disease.

CHAPTER 13

OTHER IMPORTED DISEASES

THE MORE important of the diseases which may be imported have been dealt with in other chapters. It is frequently assumed that the incoming traveller from the tropics will, if he imports a disease at all, import a tropical one. This is not so. Among the most common diseases seen in the tropics are those also seen in temperate climates: tropical diseases are frequent, but are additional. There is a vicious circle in much of disease seen in the tropics and subtropics between poor environmental health, poor nutrition and the particular disease; each factor tending to increase the effect of the other two. The traveller is much less liable to contract an infection than the average person of the country in which he has been a temporary resident. The immigrant's liability to be an unwitting carrier of disease depends very much on where he has come from and in general, apart from those diseases specially considered in other parts of this book, the amount of imported disease is not great.

Many conditions are self-limiting and, if undiscovered, may in fact not produce much ill health. A great number of diseases are not transmissible, either at all or under the conditions of temperature, sanitation, etc. obtaining in this country: these conditions are not in any way a problem from the point of view of transmissible disease and do not affect the community health other than by introducing into the community persons requiring treatment for particular conditions.

The immigrant community will have certain needs to be met by the health services and these needs may be different from that of the host community. This difference will be small in terms of the existence of special and peculiar needs but may be considerable in terms of differing amounts of various services. An increase in the relevant services will be governed by the following factors:

(a) the different age structure of the immigrant community increasing some needs (i.e. child health and maternity services.)

(b) the increased incidence of some conditions by their importation.

(c) the increased incidence of some conditions by the arrival of a population with less resistance than the indigenous population to local endemic disease.

A decreased service need will be governed by the following:

(i) the different age structure decreasing some needs (i.e. little need of geriatric and welfare services and a lesser need in respect of the diseases which commonly develop in late middle age.)

(ii) the fact that the adult males are of working age and generally of working fitness, decreasing the incidence of the chronically unfit in the immigrant as compared to the host community.

Recent surveys have shown that the balance *overall* is of a less than average requirement in the health and welfare services but that because of the above factors, severe strain on the services may result by the concentration of the need on certain aspects.

It is not the intention here to present a concise guide to imported and exotic disease: however, certain conditions need to be mentioned to put the record straight. Further details should be obtained from the appropriate textbook.

To repeat a point made previously, mention of a disease does not imply that it is common or even likely to occur.

Fevers of Unknown Origin

These are referred to in medical parlance as P.U.O. (pyrexia of unknown origin). Any person recently arriving from overseas, especially from the tropics and sub-tropics, and developing a feverish illness for which the cause is not immediately apparent, should be placed under observation, preferably in a place where medical care is experienced in the possibility of exotic disease and the necessary laboratory tests may be made. There are a whole host of causes of P.U.O. and only the minority are tropical; however, a few are serious and transmissable and due care must therefore be taken.

Typhoid and Paratyphoid

These diseases are not uncommon overseas and may present as a P.U.O. if the traveller arrives in the incubation stage of the infection. In addition, the carrier state is not uncommon in these conditions and therefore persons coming from a country where the incidence of, for example, typhoid, is relatively high, may contain a number who are typhoid carriers. It is desirable that any person who is engaged in the food handling industry in an occupation where the risk of transmitting an infection of this type is high, and who has either had a history of bowel illness or who has resided in an area in which this type of infection is known to be present to a degree more than uncommon should have a faeces and serological examination made on the same lines as that applicable to persons whose work may bring them into contact with the public water supply. This is not achieved at present, but with ever increasing amounts of food prepared by an ever decreasing number of firms, it is desirable: it must be stressed that this proposal is not confined to immigrants or specially applicable to them—it does however include them.

Poliomyelitis

The virus of poliomyelitis is very widely distributed throughout the world, especially so in those countries with a poor sanitary disposal system. The virus is an intestinal one and is excreted by those who have contracted an infection with the virus—this infection leads to involvement of the nervous system in a minority of cases. In areas where the sanitation and purity of the water supply are poor, the virus commonly infects young children while they still have enough inherited antibody to abort the infection and the incidence of paralytic poliomyelitis is extremely low. As the sanitary system improves, the infection tends to be later and the influence of maternal antibody less effective: at this stage the paralytic disease becomes more apparent. Some immigrant children arriving in this country may have previously suffered from paralytic poliomyelitis and have residual muscle weakness needing remedial treatment. Any weakness in muscular action, and any apparent imbalance in muscle strength must be reported to the relevant medical authority. If the weakness is small, it may be noted for the first time in school, especially during physical education, and teachers should be aware of this possibility.

The present state of immunization against poliomyelitis in most areas of this country is such that the general population is sufficiently protected. In addition there is no significant difference in the strains of the virus present around the world and the vaccines in current use are effective on a world-wide basis. Because distribution of the virus is world-wide, immunization against the disease needs to be maintained and this requirement is likely to exist for the foreseeable future. Due to the formerly wide distribution of the natural infection in this country, most persons over forty will have acquired immunity. Many persons will have been immunized with one of the live viral vaccines (the oral vaccine) and their immunity will be satisfactory. If no previous immunization has been carried out, then a course of three doses of the live oral vaccine at monthly intervals is desirable: if a previous immunization has been done, then a single reinforcing dose is all that is required. All persons who may come into contact with persons suffering from poliomyelitis should be immunized unless this has already been done, and to this category should be added all those who come into contact with children.

Yaws

This is a disease seen in rural areas of the tropics and sub-tropics, especially in Equatorial Africa, the Phillipines, South-east Asia, Indonesia and through the South Pacific Islands. There are also small foci of the disease in parts of the Caribbean Islands and in South America. It is a disease which is caused by an organism identical with the organism causing syphilis, but is non-venereal: it is most unlikely that transmission of the condition would occur in this country. The disease presents in children as a small papule on the skin of the body, which increases in size to form a small swelling, resembling a mole. Mild constitutional symptoms may follow in several weeks with a generalized eruption of papules. The disease is likely to be recognized quickly and treatment given.

However, a child may arrive after the development of the more recognizable primary and secondary stages of the disease and any child with bony deformities, bony tumours, unusual appearances of the skin, especially the soles of the feet, or of deformities of the fingers, should be referred for medical examination. The Wasserman test is positive in yaws and is helpful, if one keeps in mind that it is also positive in other conditions.

Trachoma

This is a chronic virus disease of the eye involving the conjunctiva and is spread by direct contact or by articles contaminated by discharges from the infected eye. The disease is chronic and infectious and frequently rapidly spreads through the family group. It is widespread in the Middle East and Asia and in parts of Africa and South America: high prevalence is associated with poor hygiene, poverty, crowded living conditions and a dry climate. Any conjunctival infection in a person, especially a child, who may have been exposed to the disease should be referred to a competent authority. It is uncommonly seen in this country, but it does occur: the chronic infection causes much scarring of the eyelids and this may affect the vision severely—at best it would involve a prolonged treatment. It could also spread among the close contacts of the sufferer.

Diphtheria

Diphtheria is a disease of worldwide distribution. It exists in two forms: the type seen in temperate climates is that of a throat infection, while in the tropics the infection is less readily apparent and cutaneous diphtheria is more common. It is unlikely that the disease will be imported. It should be remembered that the disease is still present in this country and that recent small outbreaks have been a continuation of indigenous infection: children entering this country after the age at which the usual basic immunization course of triple antigen, poliomyelitis and measles is given should receive immunization against diphtheria, tetanus, poliomyelitis and measles. To this end all families should be visited by the appropriate local health officer (usually this will be the Health Visitor) as soon after their arrival as possible to ensure that the necessary immunizations are offered.

Cholera

This disease is increasing in incidence on a world scale at the present time and is endemic in parts of India, Pakistan and Southeast Asia. The incubation period is short and, because of this, it is not a disease which has yet appeared as an importation. Because of its association with water and the high standards of the public water supply in this country, it would be most unlikely to spread if it did appear. The only difficulty it will be likely to cause to the Health Auxiliary in this country is the question of whether or not immunization against cholera should be advised for the traveller leaving this country and whether it is required under the International Sanitary Regulations.

Leprosy

This is a disease with strong emotional connotations. It is not now endemic in this country and it exists only as an importation. It is an uncommon importation but it is not rare. It often appears in a non-infectious form and although it is a transmissible disease, it is not infectious in the usual lay sense of the word. Any unexplained rash, areas of depigmentation or hyperpigmentation (that is, areas of skin darker or lighter than the patient's general shade) and thickening of the skin, or any numbness or tingling sensations in the skin should be investigated by a competent medical authority. The skin departments of the major hospitals will be aware of the disease and will be able to do the necessary tests and, if necessary, to refer the patient for an expert opinion.

Leprosy is notifiable to the Medical Officer of Health of the area in which it is diagnosed and is specially notifiable by him to the Chief Medical Officer of the Ministry of Health. This special treatment is not so much an index of the infectiousness of the disease, but rather of the necessity for skilled and prolonged treatment in order to prevent the crippling deformities which can result from delayed or imperfect treatment.

Malaria

Malaria is one of the most common diseases in the world. It is transmitted by the female Anopheline mosquito which requires a blood meal in order to lay viable eggs: the mosquito must have been previously infected by biting a person who has gametocytes of the malaria parasite in his or her blood. Malaria has been transmitted in this country in the past and could theoretically be transmitted in the future: this is very unlikely, because it is necessary for the parasite to mature in the mosquito before the mosquito becomes infective. This development would take a fortnight or more, depending on the temperature, and a life span of this length is unlikely in an Anopheline mosquito in this country. It is however possible given a source of the disease, a prolonged spell of hot weather and a marshy place capable of producing a considerable number of mosquitoes. There are four human species of malaria parasite; of these one is found in the subtropics and the other three mainly in the tropics. Those imported from the tropics would not be transmitted in this country.

A person who has been exposed repeatedly to infection with the parasite may develop resistance to the infection which enables the parasite to co-exist in the human body without causing symptoms. Under the stress of other illnesses, surgical operations or child-birth, it is possible for the disease to become clinically apparent. The parasite in its relationship with the partially immune person may exist in the red blood cell or in other tissues, mainly the liver: if it is in the clinically dormant state in the liver, a blood film will not reveal its presence.

A person who has recently come from an area in which malaria is present, and who develops a febrile illness should have a blood film taken, regardless of whether or not he has taken an anti-malaria drug prophylactically. It is important that this film is examined by a person who is technically competant to diagnose the malaria parasite.

Any person who intends to travel to a country in which malaria exists is advised to take an antimalarial drug prophylactically unless he has recently come from that area and has reason to believe that he retains some resistance to the parasite. Because of the development of drug resistance in a number of countries, it is advisable to get expert advice on a suitable antimalarial drug.

It should be realized that malaria may be dangerous. This is particularly true in the case of malignant tertian malaria (*Plasmodium falciparum*) which may kill rapidly. It is vital therefore to exclude its presence when this is a possibility.

CHAPTER 14

TUBERCULOSIS CONTROL

IN COUNTRIES with a well developed tuberculosis control service the trend in the past ten years has been for the mortality and morbidity from this disease to fall markedly in the younger age groups: in the elderly the fall has been much less and this persistance of a higher mortality and morbidity rate is more marked in the elderly male than in the elderly female. The general reduction in mortality and morbidity in the younger age groups is due to chemotherapy which has eliminated many infective cases and has prevented many from becoming infective, and to widespread BCG vaccination which has enabled large numbers of people to meet and overcome a natural infection with the tubercle bacillus. In the age group over fifty years BCG vaccination has had little influence and the discovery and the treatment of cases in this age group has become increasingly more difficult. A further factor which has delayed the falls in mortality and morbidity, particularly in countries with a developing health service, is the increasing number of drug resistant infections due mainly to inadequate treatment.

The development of active tuberculosis is influenced by four main factors (Rich 1951). These are:

(a) The magnitude of the infecting dose.
(b) The virulence of the organism.
(c) The native ability of the individual to develop a resistance to the infection.
(d) The route of entry of the infection into the body.

Rich considered that the third factor was the most important and this is certainly true in tuberculosis as found in immigrants, particularly from Asia and Africa. The magnitude of the infecting dose is in part governed by the closeness of the contact with the infecting source. Cross infection within the household is therefore more liable to produce serious disease than is casual contact within a wider social group, the infecting source remaining the same. The route of entry is also important: in u.k. it is now almost always pulmonary. Variation in the virulence of *M.tuberculosis* is probably not a major factor but it does occur: India is considered to be the main geographical area in which low virulence strains are found.

The course of tuberculosis in the individual is greatly influenced by the development of acquired resistance following primary infection whether the primary infection is natural or artificially induced by BCG vaccination. A person with a healed primary focus is considered more able to resist further infection than a non-infected person; this is the principle underlying BCG vaccination. The outcome of primary natural infection with tuberculosis with regard both to the course of the disease and to the stability of the healed primary lesion is influenced mainly by the innate resistance of the individual; this resistance is lacking in a number of races, particularly in Asia and Africa where tuberculosis is a relatively new disease. Malnutrition will also seriously affect the resistance of the body to tuberculosis and is not uncommon in these countries.

Eradication of Tuberculosis

Progress towards eradication must follow four main lines.

1. Prevention of inter-human infection by finding and controlling foci of infection in the community.

2. Raising and maintaining resistance to tuberculosis infection in all individuals.

3. Provision of adequate treatment and after-care for all persons suffering from the disease.

4. Education of the public to ensure full co-operation in Public Health measures.

(Reference: Heaf 1968, Recent advances in respiratory tuberculosis—published Churchill Ltd., 1968).

Control of Tuberculosis in an Immigrant Population

The arrival of an immigrant population may influence the local epidemiology of tuberculosis in two ways. Firstly, the arriving immigrants may include among their number those suffering from the disease, thus increasing the number of cases of disease in the general population. If these introduced cases are infectious, they are likely to give rise to other cases either among the immigrant population or among the indigenous population. Secondly, the arriving immigrants may be more susceptible to tuberculosis than the indigenous community and therefore at a higher risk to infection either from fellow immigrants or from the indigenous population.

The epidemiology of the disease may be further modified by changes in the environment of the immigrant population. For example, if they live for a time in overcrowded conditions, then the risk of spread of tuberculosis as well as other infectious diseases will be increased. The age and sex distribution of the newly arriving immigrant population is of significance. If the immigrants are mostly men of working age, they will probably live together in houses of multiple occupation where, although the room density may not reach overcrowding limits, there may nevertheless be increased risk of infection. Also the absence of women in the household may result in the men feeding less than adequately and this will predispose to infection. The 1962 Immigration Act gives power to the Port Health Authorities to require those entering as voucher holders (that is 'long-stay' immigrants) to submit to a medical examination and this medical examination includes a chest X-ray. Under the 1968 Immigration Act this provision is extended to the families and dependants of long-stay immigrants. The result of the chest X-ray is forwarded to the Medical Officer of Health of the area of the immigrant's intended destination. Whether or not an X-ray is taken, the name and intended address of the immigrant, his family and/or dependants are forwarded to the Medical Officer of Health of the receptor area.

A chest X-ray, usually taken on a 100 mm film and referred to as Mass Miniature Radiography, is a most suitable method of mass screening for pulmonary tuberculosis. As long as it is not possible for *all* long-stay immigrants *and* their families to receive a chest X-ray at the port of entry, provision must be made for this to be done at the town of arrival. If a Mass Miniature Radiography unit exists and the immigrant community can be persuaded to make use of this, it is possible to ensure the X-ray examination of the greater proportion of those arriving. The possession of a report of a recent X-ray taken in the country of origin is of limited use particularly if such a document is made into a legal requirement for entry. It is well known that certificates and documents of this nature can be forged or can be obtained by another person posing as the immigrant. It is also important that the X-ray be a recent one as, particularly in those with little resistance to tuberculosis, the disease may progress rapidly and a person suffering from active tuberculosis may well be able to produce a normal X-ray taken six months previously.

Mass Miniature Radiography is not generally used for small children as the radiation dose is higher with this method than with a machine taking a full-size film and it is better not to expose children to avoidable radiation. There is little point in X-raying Heaf negative children as part of a general population screening for tuberculosis.

It is important that as many newly arriving immigrants as possible receive a test for tuberculin sensitivity either by the Mantoux or the Heaf method. In practice the Heaf method is the most convenient and is satisfactory, provided reasonable care is taken with regard to the technique of application. By convention the front of the left forearm is the site generally used for the Heaf test. Many people from Asia will have had vaccination against smallpox done on this site and a history of a previous skin test may not in fact refer to a tuberculin test. The skin should not be cleaned with a slowly evaporating liquid such as alcohol as this will interfere with the reaction and may denature the tuberculin. Ether or acetone are satisfactory for skin cleaning and should be used in small quantities; the swab should not be 'wet'. The tuberculin used for the Heaf test is at a strength of 100,000 units per 1·0 ml. A small drop of tuberculin is applied to the dry skin and spread over the surface of the skin to form a thin film of liquid about $\frac{1}{2}$ inch in diameter. The Heaf gun is applied to this area, using a six-needle head set to penetrate 1 mm from the base plate. After application of the Heaf gun the film of liquid is allowed to dry off; this takes about 30 seconds. No dressing is necessary. A positive reaction to the Heaf test is apparent within two or three days but it is often more convenient to see the patient again in a week: this has the advantage that those with a weak or non-specific reaction to the test are less easily confused with those who have a definite positive reaction. The Heaf test and a chest X-ray are conveniently done together at the first appointment and BCG vaccination can be done at the second attendance a week later if this vaccination is indicated.

The Heaf test is recorded as negative (grade 0) or as positive (grades 1, 2, 3, 4 or 4+). Those who are Heaf negative and who have a normal chest X-ray should be offered BCG vaccination. As mentioned previously, children need not be X-rayed as a routine screening measure: they need only be Heaf tested at the first attendance and an X-ray examination arranged later if the Heaf test is positive. BCG vaccination can be given to a Heaf negative child without first obtaining a normal chest X-ray.

The result of the Heaf test is recorded according to the scheme shown in Figure 4.

Reactions to tuberculin may be non-specific; that is, due to mycobacteria other than the one causing tuberculosis in man. Generally speaking these non-specific reactions tend to be mild and a definite grade 2 reaction and grade 3, 4 and 4+ reactions can be assumed to indicate specific sensitivity due to a previous infection with tubercle bacilli responsible for disease in man. A weak reaction due to sensitivity to other mycobacteria does not indicate resistance to the human type of the infection and a person with such a tuberculin reaction should not be denied BCG vaccination. An immigrant may have little natural resistance to tuberculous infection and the interpretation of tuberculin tests and the subsequent decision with regard to BCG vaccination must be approached with care. Some of the reactions causing difficulty in interpretation are illustrated in Figure 5.

BCG vaccination is by intradermal injection of 0·1 ml of freshly prepared BCG vaccine. The injection can be done by the standard method using a tuberculin syringe and a fine intradermal needle or by the use of the intrajet or similar injection gun which, by using a very fine jet under high pressure, injects 0·1 ml of the vaccine without the need of a needle. It is important that the gun

NEGATIVE

No reaction:
faint sign of puncture marks.

POSITIVE

Grade 1

Reaction to at least 4 punctures.
Induration 1mm. in diameter
around each puncture.

Grade 2

Induration 2mm. in diameter
around each puncture: slight
oedema joining all or some
areas of induration.

Grade 3

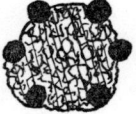

More intensive induration.
More than 2mm. in diameter
with oedema and induration
between puncture marks
forming a ring pattern.

Grade 4

Complete disc of induration
5-10mm. in diameter.

Grade 4+

Disc of induration more than
10mm. in diameter. May be
ulceration in addition.

Fig. 4

used be properly maintained and that it has been adequately tested
before being marketed as it is essential that the vaccine is not

injected subcutaneously: if subcutaneous injection occurs, a severe local reaction is likely and this may need treatment with anti-tuberculous drugs applied locally. An injection gun is most useful when a considerable number of injections have to be given and for BCG vaccination of young children. It is doubtful if much

NEGATIVE

Sign of puncture marks with surrounding slight inflammation. No induration.

WEAK POSITIVE: probably non-specific

Induration of less than 1 mm. around each puncture mark.

POSITIVE: probably specific

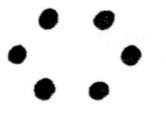

Induration definite: at least 1 mm. in diameter and felt easily with the finger.

Induration definite and marked but present only on one side of the puncture marks—indicates Heaf gun not correctly applied.

Fig. 5

benefit acrues from giving BCG to the elderly—that is over fifty years of age—but one does not often find people of this age Heaf negative. Any BCG vaccine unused at the end of the session should be discarded.

Those giving a strongly positive reaction to the Heaf test should be followed up and fresh X-ray taken six months later. The patient's general practitioner should be informed of the result of the Heaf test as there appears to be an increased incidence of non-pulmonary tuberculosis developing in this group of patients. At the time of the second attendance, when the result of the Heaf test is read, the patient should be asked about his general health as it is possible that symptoms of extrapulmonary tuberculosis may be present at that time. The patient's general practitioner should be informed at all times of the result of X-rays, Heaf tests and also of any vaccinations given.

The patient should be told whether or not his X-ray is satisfactory. This information should be given; firstly, because it is the patient's right to know and secondly, to encourage good relations between medical staff and the immigrant. It is of prime importance that these good relations be maintained, particularly in the early days of an immigrant's arrival in a strange community. It is important that the tuberculosis control clinic operates smoothly and with flexibility. This is usually easier if the X-ray facilities are outside the hospital and not liable to interruption or delay by medical and surgical emergencies. Sessions should be timed to coincide with the most convenient time for attendance of the client and a choice should be given by holding sessions at different times. It should be remembered that wives may not be accustomed to attend clinics without their husbands and thus may be able to attend only in the evening. As the immigrant men have come to this country to work, most will be at work and unavailable to escort their families during working hours. An open access type of session is best and will result in good attendances once the confidence of the immigrant community has been obtained. It must be the aim of all staff working with immigrant communities and in particular the newly arrived immigrants to obtain and to hold the confidence of that community: this can only be done by deserving such confidence and not losing it through thoughtlessness or carelessness.

Notification of the arriving immigrant and of his family may be forthcoming from the port Health Authority at the port of entry. However, it is not unusual for an arriving immigrant to visit friends or relatives in another town before going on to his final destination. In these cases notifications of arrival will be likely to arrive with the Medical Officer of Health at the 'transit area' rather than in the 'arrival area'. Some Authorities have arranged with the local Executive Council for the notification of newly arrived immigrants registering for the first time with a family doctor. Families with children of school age will be registering their children for schooling and this may be a method of contacting not only the child but the rest of the family as well. Given good relations between staff and the immigrant, it is not difficult to find out if other members of the family have had a skin test and X-ray. All women attending ante-natal clinics should have an enquiry directed to them with regard to the skin testing and chest X-ray of other members of their family. They themselves should be Heaf-tested and a chest X-ray should be taken in the fourth, fifth or sixth month of pregnancy. If they have any symptoms or abnormal physical signs which might indicate pulmonary tuberculosis, then a chest X-ray should be taken whatever the stage of pregnancy: in the pregnant women a full size film rather than a miniature one is taken and the rest of the body is screened against radiation.

Tuberculosis control does not end with the identification of the imported case and the protection of the Heaf negative patient by BCG vaccination. The immigrant may by virtue of his race be more susceptible to tuberculosis infection than the indigenous population even when he has acquired a degree of resistance either naturally or by BCG vaccination. It is important therefore that facilities should exist for the X-ray of all those showing minimal symptoms, and the family doctor should be able to refer such patients for mass miniature radiography easily and quickly. A general practitioner practising in areas where there is a considerable number of immigrants will be aware of the advisability for a chest X-ray to be taken in all those with minimal symptoms: it is important for the field worker to encourage immigrants to seek the aid of their family doctors if they are suffering from cough or fever of more than two weeks' duration or of loss of weight.

Tuberculosis in the Asian and African is more rapidly progressive than in the European and symptoms of disease are usually more readily apparent. Nevertheless, symptoms may be ignored either because the patient is frightened of falling ill or because he does not consider them significant. Cases may be picked up by mobile mass miniature radiography if this is made available at the place of work.

Apart from individual susceptibility to tuberculosis, the incidence of the infection will vary according to the chances that a person has of coming into contact with an infected case. Community customs are therefore important: if the men are mobile while the women tend to remain at home, then the men will be satisfactorily covered by mobile mass miniature radiography at the place of work. If infection is introduced into the home environment, the women will tend to form the 'closed community' type of transmission of infection and will need to have special arrangements made for their X-ray screening sessions for early detection of tuberculosis.

The basis of control remains as follows:

(i) Identification of the imported case as soon as possible after arrival. Treatment of this case removing the source of infection from the community.

(ii) Identification of the susceptible (Heaf negative) person who is then offered the protection of BCG vaccination.

(iii) Early referral for chest X-ray of those with minimal symptoms.

(iv) Availability of routine chest X-rays for such immigrants who may, because of their genetic constitution be at greater risk than the average member of the community. Mobile mass miniature radiography at the mill or factory, chest X-ray of the women through ante-natal clinics and X-ray of the school leaver are important here.

(v) Identification of those in whom the disease may not yet be apparent on chest X-ray or who may be developing extra-pulmonary tuberculosis (Grade 4 Heaf reactors).

The discovery of a case of tuberculosis will set in motion the full contact tracing procedure: the aim of this is to find the source of the infection, to detect other infected persons and to protect with

BCG vaccination those who are found to have no natural resistance to the disease. The method used is to trace and list all the contacts of the newly discovered case: these contacts will be found in the person's household, in his workplace and in visitors to his household. If he has regular social meetings with other groups of people then these too should be regarded as contacts—for example, fellow members of the same club, committee, etc. Much will depend on whether or not the discovered case could have been infectious. If he could have transmitted the disease to others then *all* contacts must be traced, Heaf tested and X-rayed: if they have a negative reaction to the Heaf test then, provided the X-ray is satisfactory, they should be offered BCG vaccination. It is, except in very young children, necessary to X-ray before giving BCG as if the person is suffering from tuberculosis and has not yet had time to develop a positive reaction to the Heaf test, BCG vaccination might cause the tuberculosis infection to progress faster: this danger, however, is much less since the advent of effective chemotherapeutic drugs. If the discovered case is not infectious, then contact tracing is aimed at the discovery of the source and then the examination of contacts of that source.

In this type of investigation a number of persons are found who give a negative reaction to the Heaf Test. They are not infected and perhaps not in this particular instance liable to have been infected but are nevertheless shown to be lacking in general resistance to the disease. These persons should always be offered BCG vaccination and the advantage of this made clear to them.

Tuberculosis is an important infectious disease. Morbidity from tuberculosis is considerable and it is still an important cause of death. The arrival of an immigrant community from areas where the incidence of tuberculosis may be higher or whose resistance to the infection is lower than that of the host community gives rise to major problems. These problems are not insoluble and the action outlined here will be adequate in controlling the spread of the infection. Treatment and history-taking will be complicated by language difficulties, but a suitable interpreter or, better still, a medical auxiliary speaking the immigrants' language and understanding their customs can resolve these difficulties.

A newly arrived immigrant may, with considerable justification, be extremely fearful of entering hospital where both familiar food and familiar language may be absent. The patient's family may decide to remove him or her from hospital against medical advice, and this will make further relations between family and medical staff more difficult. Treatment may have to be modified in certain cases and it may be better for antibiotic treatment to be given at home under the day to day supervision of a firm but friendly district nurse or health visitor, rather than that the interfamily and family-doctor relationships be considerably upset by removal of the patient to hospital. The object of treatment is to cure the patient and guard against further transmission of the disease: if this can be effected at home satisfactorily, then this may be the best solution.

If tuberculosis is discovered, then the population in which it is found must be considered to be at risk and must be given maximum protection. This, of course, is a generalization and does not apply only to immigrant groups. If there is a group in whom the disease is particularly liable to spread by virtue of living conditions or by the lack of general resistance then this group must be awarded a high priority in measures designed to control of the infections. The existence of such a priority grading does not, however, detract in any way from the necessity of dealing with the infection in the population at large; it merely indicates the methods appropriate to particular circumstances.

CHAPTER 15

VENEREAL DISEASE

IN SPITE of the general decrease in both mortality and morbidity from infectious diseases in the past two decades, the incidence of venereal disease has remained high and has increased in recent years. In 1966 the reported incidence of gonorrhoea in England and Wales was 37,483 cases and the number of reported cases of infectious syphilis was 1,819. In 1967 the incidence was 41,829 cases of gonorrhoea and 1,732 cases of syphilis. In 1967, in the age range 16–19, one in 500 boys and one in 440 girls were known to have contracted gonorrhoea: one in 15,700 boys and one in 32,300 girls contracted syphilis. In the age range 20–24, one in 190 men and one in 450 women had contracted gonorrhoea, while one in 7,900 men and one in 23,200 women had contracted syphilis.

The Ministry of Health memorandum of November 1968 summarized the main epidemiological factors, common to both gonorrhoea and syphilis, of the recent increase in incidence as follows:

(a) An apparent increase in promiscuity, both heterosexual and homosexual.

(b) Asymptomatic infections, especially in women and passive male homosexuals.

(c) Failure to trace sources of infection and to bring them for treatment.

(d) A recent influx of immigrants, who seldom introduce infection but who contract it in disproportionate numbers after arrival.

(e) An increase of infection, especially of syphilis, imported by travellers, reflecting the world-wide increase in prevalence.

The high infectivity, short incubation period and development of resistant strains are additional factors relating to gonorrhoea.

Factor (d) above is the reason for the inclusion of a chapter on venereal disease in this book. The problem of the unattached male and the associated rise in the prevalence of venereal disease has been a common problem for centuries. The increased incidence of venereal disease in and around military camps is well known and has exercised the minds of many military medical officers and commanders.

It has been found that immigrant males, especially those living in groups in a single household, have been subjected to a type of high pressure sales technique by local prostitutes visiting the household. The rise in England and Wales in the incidence of 'exotic' venereal diseases, relatively common in some areas of the tropics and sub-tropics, has been small and has not been much of a problem. The immigrant is at greater risk to infection when he is separated from his family and also because he may be naïve and less resistant to the persuasion from a type of prostitute more liable to be infected than the average one.

Venereal Disease and the Law

It is useful to summarize the law as it applies to venereal diseases and also as some of it has applied in the past.

Under the Contagious Disease Acts of 1864, 1866 and 1869, prostitutes and those who were alleged to be prostitutes could be compelled to undergo a medical examination and, if this showed that they were suffering from venereal disease, could be compelled to receive treatment. Under the 1866 and 1869 Acts, brothels were licensed and prostitutes were registered. These three Acts were repealed in 1886.

Under the Public Health (Ophthalmia Neonatorum) Regulations of 1914 and 1926 notification of this disease was required to be made to the Medical Officer of Health. The later Regulations required notification to be by the medical practitioner treating the case: the midwife is required to call in medical aid for this disease under the Midwives Act. The Public Health (Venereal Diseases) Regulations of 1916 put the responsibility on major health authorities to provide free diagnosis, treatment and prevention, and to set up special centres for this. Laboratory services were to be provided free of charge and hospital beds were to be provided for the treatment of certain venereal diseases. The Venereal

Diseases Act of 1917 made it illegal for other than registered medical practitioners to treat venereal diseases and also made advertisement of drugs and treatments for venereal disease illegal. The National Health Service Act of 1946 laid upon Regional Hospital Boards the responsibility of provision of treatment of venereal disease at clinics and hospitals and upon Local Authorities the responsibility for publicity, health education and care.

In the first world war, under the Defence of the Realm Act, Regulation 40D, it was an offence punishable by a prison sentence of up to six months for a prostitute to practise her profession if suffering from venereal disease. In the second world war, under Regulation 33B of 1942, if a Medical Officer of Health received a complaint of infection from two people regarding the source of that infection, then the infected source could be compelled to receive treatment. Many Local Authorities did not follow this practice but authorized the Medical Officer of Health to approach notified contacts of venereal disease informally on receipt of a single notification. Most Local Authorities have continued this practice, which has been found by long experience to be preferable to compulsory powers of examination and treatment. A private members bill currently before the House of Commons seeks to return to powers of compulsory examination and treatment on the lines of Regulation 33B: most of those with experience in the treatment and control of venereal disease would consider that such legislation would make treatment and particularly prevention more difficult and would be a positive hindrance.

In a memorandum dated November 1968 the Ministry of Health considered that the most important method of control was the rapid tracing of the contact and that this speed should be the maximum possible. The memorandum also emphasized that complete confidentiality be maintained between the patient and the doctor by restricting medical records to those who needed to refer to them and who were aware of their duties with regard to maintaining secrecy. The principle behind this memorandum has been put into administrative effect by the introduction of The National Health Service (Venereal Diseases) Regulations of 1968; these amend previous regulations and ensure that all information from the hospital service regarding persons treated or examined for venereal disease remains confidential except for the purpose of communicating to a medical practitioner or a person working under his direction such information as may be necessary for the treatment and prevention of the spread of the disease.

The Street Offences Act of 1959 has effectively taken soliciting by prostitutes off the street and public places but has increased the incidence of pimping and the call-girl system. No legislation has been found to be effective in the prevention of prostitution.

Venereal diseases are not 'notifiable diseases' within the provisions of the Infectious Diseases Regulations and notification is not compulsory under English law. The system of informal notification works well: the only loop-hole is a possible failure by a doctor treating a patient outside the sphere of operation of the special treatment clinic to notify informally and thus fail to set in motion the standard contact tracing procedure. As the laboratory tests, etc., required in effective treatment are specialized, it is doubtful whether many doctors would consider themselves able to treat venereal diseases without the aid of specialist advice and technical aids. The Venereal Diseases Regulations of 1968 make obligatory the provision of information by the Hospital Services—who are responsible for the provision of diagnostic and treatment facilities under the National Health Service Act of 1946—to those who legitimately need to have such information: generally this is the Local Health Authority.

In most legislation, venereal disease has been specifically defined as comprising syphilis, gonorrhoea and chancroid (soft sore).

Control of Venereal Disease

In order to treat and prevent venereal disease, it is essential to obtain and to maintain complete confidentiality between patient or prospective patient and the medical staff. This must not only be maintained but must be seen to have been maintained. It is also necessary to have facilities for diagnosing, including adequate examination equipment, adequate laboratory aids and the means for continuing treatment until a cure can be pronounced. The Venereal Diseases Act of 1917 made treatment by other than a registered medical practitioner an offence and this was applicable

K

to areas in which the Venereal Disease Regulation of 1916 had been applied to provide facilities for diagnosis and treatment. The provision of the 1917 Act have long since applied to the whole country and the suppression of the quack has been of considerable benefit. The provision of the Act relating to advertisements may still need to be invoked occasionally.

Routine ante-natal examination

Routine serological tests on all pregnant women is a standard practice in ante-natal clinics. Routine installation of a bacteriocidal agent or antibiotic into the conjunctival sac of the infant soon after birth as described and introduced by Credé is not now standard practice in this country. Routine ante-natal care and routine careful observation of the new-born remains a vital part of the prevention of venereal infection, both congenital and acquired.

Premarital Examination

Pre-marital examination for venereal disease, often combined with pre-marriage guidance and health education has not found much support in this country, although there is considerable support for the education and guidance. It should be noted at this stage that no serological test exists which distinguishes venereal syphilis from non-venereal syphilis and that the test may give a false positive, and in some diseases often does.

Health education ranks high among the general methods of control. It has most chance of success in the reasonably intelligent young who may, assisted by alcohol and the local climate of opinion, see no harm in the casual liaison. Health education should also aim at persuading the infected or those who may become infected to obtain skilled advice and treatment at the earliest opportunity: the confidential nature of the whole procedure needs to be stressed and re-stressed.

It is of course true that there is a greater acceptance of sexual liaisons outside marriage as 'normal' at the present time than twenty-five years ago. This has resulted in the spread of venereal disease in groups of the population that would not have been considered to be at much risk a generation ago. Extra-marital unions, if otherwise 'constant', will have no effect on the spread of venereal diseases if neither partner suffers from the disease: it is the promiscuous and casual sexual union which is the epidemiologically significant factor in the continuing spread of the disease.

It is outside the scope of this book to deal with the prevention of venereal disease by instruction and education particularly of the adolescent and young adult, on the dangers of sexual promiscuity. It is, however, not specially relevant when undertaking this task to bemoan the sins of the present age: such an approach is doomed to be the failure that it deserves. Both the Marriage Guidance Council and the Family Planning Association issue material to aid health education in this field and reference should be made to this when preparing to take part in such instruction. It is essential that the right person is used to lead teaching groups and discussions on this subject and that the teaching material is carefully prepared beforehand.

The unmarried mother may be suffering from venereal disease. If this occurs, two separate problems are involved; firstly the treatment of the disease and the identification of the source of the infection and possibly other contacts in order to control the spread of the disease, and secondly, the care for the mother and her child.

Physical Methods of Prevention of Infection

Prevention of infection by other than health education aimed at causing the recipient not to take the risk does not offer a great chance of success. The provision of condoms has been a common practice in armies and also the provision of a preventive centre where a man who has run the risk of infection may, under medical auxiliary supervision, wash and irrigate the affected part with a solution with some anti-bacterial powers. It is rather doubtful if these remedies prevent much infection: the use of a condom is generally effective in preventing gonorrhoea, less effective in preventing syphilis and not at all sure in preventing lympho-granuloma venerum or granuloma inguinale. The system has little application in civilian practice.

Contact Tracing

Preventive methods used and suggested in the past have been various and not very effective: contact tracing is the keystone of epidemiological control and in it lies the best hope of breaking the chain of infection. The aim of contact tracing is to obtain information, from those diagnosed as having a venereal infection, which leads to the identification of their sexual contacts and the persuasion of these contacts to attend for examination and treatment. It is sometimes possible to trace contacts of contacts and although this is generally impossible in the case of the prostitute, it may be possible in the less promiscuous amateur. It is of course essential that all contact tracing is confidential and is recognized as such by those for whom the service is intended. Nothing must be done to break or to appear to break this confidence: to do so would be professionally most improper as well as highly inefficient.

The patient may be in the United Kingdom but the contact overseas. In such a case information is conveyed to the Ministry of Health who transmit it to the Port Health Authority of the country concerned who will either deal with the tracing themselves or refer it to the appropriate medical authority. If these circumstances are reversed, for example in the case of a seaman visiting this country with his ship, then information would be received by the Ministry of Health who pass it on to the Medical Officer of Health or to the professional head of the Venereal Diseases Clinic in the area concerned. All information is passed in the strictest confidence.

Usually both case and contact are in this country and are often in the same area. If another area is involved, then information would be passed by the interviewer to the Medical Officer of Health or other appropriate medical authority of the area of the suspected contact. Interviews are carried out in a room which is private and it is important that the interviewer is not impeded by visitors, visiting colleagues or the telephone during the interview with the case or contact. The patient's name is kept secret and is not revealed to the contact unless in very rare circumstances this is necessary *and* authorized by the patient. The patient may be given 'contact slips' and these are presented by the contact who has been persuaded to attend at the appropriate clinic. These slips are successful where a regular consort is involved, but if the union is casual the rate of success is small. The interview and the completion of the type of contact report as illustrated (Fig. 6) will be the main method of contact detection. Once the contact is identified, either completely or in part, he or she will then have to be approached. This can only be done by a person who by personality and by professional competance is qualified for this task. The senior health visitor, experienced in this field, is the person who most often qualifies for the post. When the contact has been traced it is important that the result of the tracing process is recorded: this is best done on the type of return illustrated. (The examples of the contact form and contact tracing report are taken from the Ministry of Health's memorandum on Contact Tracing in the Control of Venereal Disease, November 1968, to which further reference may be made.)

The main difficulty in dealing with immigrant communities will be found in the language barrier. An interpreter must have some knowledge of what the contact tracing procedure involves, a basic knowledge of the technical terms involved, so that the translation will be meaningful in both directions. The interpreter must also have the right personality and must practice the 'professional' secrecy which is so vital. The selection of the right person must therefore be approached with great care; the ability to speak the languages required being only one of the qualifications.

Some difficulty may be found in getting the right description from the patient, especially with reference to 'slim, thin, medium, plump or stout', 'blonde or brunette, fair, red or dark' etc. A do-it-yourself identikit can be prepared by cutting suitable pictures out of magazines and gluing them on a board.

A description of the various venereal diseases will not be given in this book. Reference may be made to the standard textbooks for this.

IN CONFIDENCE

Special Clinic Contact Report   ref. no.

To: The Medical Officer of Health:

_____

A patient at this clinic under treatment for... of approximately   days/weeks/months duration has disclosed IN STRICT CONFIDENCE the information overleaf about an alleged contact.

Signed......................................

Designation
for Director

....Special Clinic

_____

Address ....

                    date 196

_____

Note:—To fill in this form put ticks against the relevant features, and comment in the adjacent spaces. For example, in the box for hair style, a tick might be put against "long" and "pigtail" written in the space at the right of the box.

_____

Fig. 6a

IN CONFIDENCE
PART I

Name and nickname... Male/Female

Address ....

Age: years.   Nationality: Occupation:

Single   Married   Separated   Widowed   Children

DESCRIPTION

COLOUR	white		coloured		half-caste	

HAIR COLOUR			HAIR STYLE		
fair				long	
red				short	
brunette				medium	
black					

HEIGHT	tall		short		medium		approx. ht.		ft.		ins.

BUILD	thin		slim		medium		plump		stout	

FACE			MAKE-UP		
round				heavy	
				moderate	
long				none	

EYES	blue		grey		other colour	
	green		brown		glasses	

TEETH			NAILS		
even		bad		long		varnished (colour)
uneven		missing		short		
good		false		bitten		

SPEECH			HABITS		
english		foreign		non-smoker		drug-taker
accent				smoker		

DRESS					
well dressed		hat		coat	
ordinary		hatless		leather jacket	
unkempt		headscarf		trouser suit	
suit		skirt			
costume		jumper			
slacks		blouse			
jeans		frock			
jacket		cardigan			

FOOTWEAR	high heels		boots		low heels		stockings	

ACCESSORIES	rings		bracelet		handbag		
	earrings		necklace		watch		

TYPE OF CONTACT	co-habiting		pick-up		other	
	friend		prostitute			

PLACE OF ENCOUNTER	public house	dance hall	cafe	home	cinema	club	bus or rly. station	park	party	taxi	street

ADDRESS

PLACE OF EXPOSURE	hotel	his home	her home	friend's home	car	park	street	taxi	brothel

ADDRESS

SOLICITATION	yes		FEE PAID		Enter any other information on the next page
	no				

Fig. 6b

Other information..

....

....

....

....

....

....

....

....

....

....

....

....

....

....

STRICTLY CONFIDENTIAL   **CONTACT TRACING REPORT**

PART II

To the Physician-in-Charge
Address of Special Clinic...

....

Patient's Ref. No.................................../*C.I. Form No..

From.. *Medical Officer of Health/
                                                    Director of Special Clinic

Date....................................

The person (contact) described in Part I was:

    (a) Located
          Not located

    (b) Examined at ....
          Not examined

    (c) Already under treatment
          Brought under treatment

    (d) Infected with ....
          Not infected

*delete as applicable.

Fig. 6c

Signed.............................. Designation...................... date...............19...

CHAPTER 16

HELMINTHIC INFESTATION

HELMINTHS are parasitic worms frequently found in man and animals. There are three large groups: roundworms (Nemathelminthes), flatworms (Platyhelminthes) and leeches (Hirudinea). The flatworms include the tapeworms (Cestoda) and flukes (Trematoda). Relatively few of the many species of helminths parasitize humans.

Parasitic worms are harboured by hundreds of millions of people, the great majority of whom live in under-developed parts of the world. Children are often infested and of those of school age recently arriving in this country from West Pakistan and the northern states of India, about 20 per cent had significant degrees of infestation. An even greater proportion of children from East Pakistan and from the West Indies were affected.

Mature worms develop from their eggs in ways that differ according to the species of helminth and the particular life-cycles determine methods of spread. Five types occur, namely:

1. directly infective
2. soil transmitted
3. food transmitted
4. arthropod transmitted
5. snail transmitted

The common species of helminths infecting man will be described under these five headings.

Directly infective, i.e. those worms whose eggs or larvae are infective when passed in the faeces or deposited at the anus. The best known example is the threadworm, *Enterobius vermicularis*, which is frequently harboured by children in all parts of the world. Male and female threadworms live attached to the mucosa of the caecum. They look like thin, white cotton threads, the female being about 1 cm long and the male rather less than half this size. Gravid female worms migrate to the anus and deposit many thousands of eggs on the perianal skin, usually at night. Irritation is caused and as a result of scratching, the child's fingers are contaminated with eggs which may then be transferred to his mouth either directly or on food. In addition, eggs may adhere to clothing, bedding or other objects. Following ingestion of an egg, the larva hatches in the duodenum and migrates to the caecum where it develops into a mature worm in two to four weeks.

The eggs are not often found on microscopical examination of faeces but can be detected in cellotape swabs of the perianal skin. Several members of a household may be infected simultaneously and examination of all household contacts is desirable.

Many worms can be present in any individual child and his health may be adversely affected by perianal soreness, tiredness and irritability. Occasionally threadworms may cause inflammation of the appendix.

Another example of a parasitic worm whose eggs are infective when passed in the faeces, is the dwarf tapeworm, *Hymenolepis nana*. This parasite is 12 to 20 mms long and attaches itself to the mucosa of the small intestine by a series of hooks and four suckers on the scolex or head. The rest of the tapeworm consists of over a hundred tiny segments each containing both male and female reproductive organs. Most of the terminal segments are occupied by eggs which are released into the faeces by disintegration of the segments.

The dwarf tapeworm is thought to affect over 20 million people in the world and is most common in the Indian Sub-Continent, the Soviet Transcaucasus, the Mediterranean basin and Central and South America. In some parts of these regions more than 10 per cent of children, most commonly those in the age group five to nine years, harbour the parasite. It rarely occurs in the first year of life or in adults.

Spread of the infestation is due to the transfer of eggs from contaminated hands to the mouth in a fashion similar to that of threadworm, (it has been suggested that rodents, which can also harbour the parasite, or insect intermediate hosts may play a part in its transmission), and it is particularly likely to occur in the families of infected children, in children's homes and other places where there is close contact of infested with susceptible children.

Most children infested with the dwarf tapeworm suffer no ill effects but a proportion do complain of abdominal discomfort, general symptoms such as headache and occasionally it may result in epileptiform convulsions. Treatment is difficult in that although anthelmintic drugs may eliminate eggs from the stools for several months, recurrence of ova excretion is frequent.

Soil transmitted helminths are not immediately infective when passed in the faeces but become infective after a period of development in soil. This group contains several parasites important in humans, an example being the roundworm, *Ascaris lumbricoides*. It is widely distributed in the world, particularly where sanitary facilities are inadequate and it is estimated that over 600 million people are infested. (The infection is particularly common in young children.)

The mature worm is about 25 cms long and $\frac{1}{2}$ cm in diameter, the female worm being rather larger than the male. It normally lives in the small intestine where the female worm lays approximately two hundred thousand minute eggs each day. The eggs have a tough outer coat and are resistant to most environmental influences. In warm countries they develop within two to three weeks and become infective to any individuals who may swallow them as a result of soil contamination of their water or food supplies.

Following ingestion, the egg hatches in the small intestine and a tiny larva which escapes burrows into the intestinal wall, gets into the circulation, is carried to the right side of the heart and eventually to the lungs where further development takes place. Migration then takes place from the lung, up the trachea, down the oesophagus and through the stomach, finally arriving in the small intestine where development to the mature form is completed.

Many children with roundworm infections are unaware of their presence but allergic manifestations such as asthma are frequent and during the migration of larvae through the lungs, pneumonia, which is occasionally fatal, can occur. When many worms are present they may cause abdominal pain and jaundice may result from migration of worms into the biliary tract. Mature worms may be vomited by an infested child.

Eradication of the infestation is usually effected without

difficulty by giving specific anthelminthic treatment, and provided that there is no opportunity for re-infection the child remains free from the parasite. Prevention of re-infection in areas where the condition is prevalent is dependent upon high standards of personal and culinary hygiene and the availability of a safe water supply.

Another soil transmitted helminth often found in association with *Ascaris lumbricoides* is the whipworm, *Trichuris trichiura*. It is a small worm about 30 to 50 mms long, the front part resembling a fine hair and this bores into the wall of the intestine so that it lies underneath the mucosal surface. The remainder is much thicker and hangs free inside the intestine, most commonly in the caecum, the lower part of the small intestine and the ascending colon.

Female worms pass several thousand eggs each day and these complete their development in water or damp soil after about three weeks. Whipworm eggs, like those of the roundworm, are very resistant to most environmental conditions and may remain alive for a considerable period of time. Man is infected by swallowing the fully developed eggs as a result of contamination of his drinking water or food.

A small proportion of children with whipworm suffer from abdominal disturbances and loss of appetite and some with heavy degrees of infestation may have anaemia associated with passing blood in their stools. The majority of children are not troubled by it however, and since the medication used to expel the worm has unpleasant side effects there may be no justification for treatment of light asymptomatic infestations.

The most common helminth found in immigrant children in England during the past few years has been hookworm, the two main types *Ancylostmoa duodenale* and *Necator americanus* being distinguished by microscopical examination of the mouth of the parasite.

The former hookworm is prevalent in Asia, particularly India, and the latter type, as the name would suggest, is more common in Central and South America. The total of hookworm infestations in the world is estimated to be about 457 million.

The worms are about 1 cm long and 0·3 to 0·4 mms in breadth. They are attached by their mouths to the lining mucosa in the upper part of the small intestine. The female worm lays rather fragile, oval shaped eggs which are passed in the faeces of the host. In places where the climate is warm and the soil is sandy and moist the eggs hatch after about forty-eight hours. A larval form escapes which develops very rapidly and becomes infective within five to ten days. Man is infected by the larva penetrating the skin, particularly of the feet, in societies where shoes are not worn.

Having penetrated the skin, larvae migrate into the blood vessels and are carried through the right side of the heart to the lungs where further development takes place. After entering the respiratory tract, they migrate up the trachea into the throat and are swallowed. On reaching the duodenum they attach themselves to the wall and following the ingestion of blood become sexually mature within a few weeks.

Light degrees of infestation with hookworm probably have no very significant effect on the health of the host but a loss of blood does occur and in heavier degrees of infestation is significant, leading to anaemia with resultant lethargy, mental apathy and delayed physical development. In environments where reinfection from soil does not take place, children rid themselves of hookworms within about four years. They can also be rapidly and efficiently eliminated by use of an anthelminthic which can be given in a single dose.

Another parasite similar to the hookworms described is *Strongyloides stercoralis* which is fairly common in warm, moist climates and infests an estimated 35 million people throughout the world.

It is a very fine, thread-like worm, about 2 mms. long, which lives under the mucosal lining of the intestine where it lays its eggs. When they hatch larvae escape into the lumen of the intestine and are passed in the faeces. They may then develop into a generation living freely in the soil or alternatively, may become directly infective to man. The larvae penetrate the skin of the feet in a way similar to hookworm larvae or may gain access to the body by contamination of food. On reaching the blood stream they are carried through the right side of the heart to the lungs and, like hookworms, migrate up the trachea and down the oesophagus before they finally mature and burrow into the mucosal lining of the intestine.

Generally the infestation produces few symptoms but it may result in abdominal pain, digestive disturbances or signs of pneumonia when larvae migrate through the lungs. Treatment is rather more difficult than with hookworm, the advised therapy being rather toxic to the patient. It is also significant that reinfection of children may lead to massive infestation with consequent serious effects on health.

Food transmitted helminths, i.e. helminths with an infective stage in the flesh of fish or mammals consumed by man. The best known examples are the beef and pork tapeworms, *Taenia saginata* and *Taenia solium,* respectively. About 39 million people, mostly in Africa and the U.S.S.R., harbour the former and about 3 million people, mostly in Asia, are infested with the latter parasite.

Taenia attaches to the upper part of the small intestine of man by four suckers and a row of hooks on the tiny head, or scolex, in the case of *Taenia solium* and by four suckers alone in the case of *Taenia saginata.* The bodies of both adult worms are segmented and may be several feet in length. Each segment, or proglottid, contains both male and female sex organs and the terminal segments contain many eggs. The segments break off and are passed in the faeces. These disintegrate in soil, releasing eggs which are infective to cattle. Bovine infections result from grazing on contaminated pastures. After hatching, larvae migrate to the muscle of the animal where further development takes place. Man is infected by eating the raw or undercooked flesh.

Arthropod-transmitted, i.e. parasites requiring an intermediate host such as flies or mosquitos for development of the infective stage. Important examples are the filarial worms, of which several species frequently infest man. It is estimated that about 189 million people in the world, particularly in South East Asia, the Equatorial belt of Africa and South America, are infested with the filarial worm, *Wuchereria bancrofti.* In addition, about 20 million people, mostly in Africa, harbour the filarial worm *Onchocerca volvulus* and about 13 million in West Africa have *Loa loa.*

Adult filarids are thread-like worms, most of them having a length of about 3 cms. They parasitize subcutaneous or lymphatic tissues and instead of laying eggs produce larvae called microfilaria. These get into the circulatory system and a point of interest

is that the microfilaria of *Wuchereria bancrofti* begin to appear in
the peripheral blood stream in the early evening, reach a maximum
about midnight and afterwards gradually decrease. Development of
microfilaria depends upon ingestion by one of several species of
mosquitoes which feed on human blood. The larvae penetrate the
insects' gut and migrate to its thoracic muscles where they grow
and mature into infective forms. These move subsequently to
the proboscis where they remain until the mosquito or fly has
another meal. They then break out of the proboscis onto the skin
of the new host and are able to enter through any break in the
surface.

Maturation to the adult form takes place during the ensuing
months. In the case of *Wuchereria bancrofti* this occurs in the
lymphatic tissues which may become acutely inflamed. Repeated
attacks of lymphangitis lead to scarring and obstruction of the
lymphatic vessels and cause gross thickening of the skin and
swelling of the parts of the body beyond the obstruction. In
addition to lymphangitis, *Onchocerca volvulus* also causes painless
swellings under the skin. It is characteristic of this parasite that the
microfilaria tend to cause blindness by migrating to the eyes and
to the optic nerve. The filarial worm, *Loa loa* is found under the
skin where it may cause 'Calabar swellings' in various parts of the
body and may similarly be seen during the course of migration
across the eye.

Anthelminthic drugs may kill microfilaria in the circulation but
are less certain in their action against adult worms, treatment of
which is often difficult.

Snail-transmitted, i.e. parasites needing to invade certain snails
in order to complete their development. The most important
examples are the blood flukes causing Schistosomiasis, there being
three main types in the human host. *Schistosomiasis japonicum*
occurs in South East Asia and affects about 46 million people,
Schistosomiasis haematobium occurs in Egypt and East Africa and
affects about 39 million people, and *Schistosomiasis mansoni* occurs
in equatorial Africa, the West Indies and parts of South America
and affects an estimated 29 million people.

The adult flukes live in the veins of the lower abdomen in the
case of *Schistosomiasis haematobium,* mostly in the plexus of veins

proximate to the urinary bladder, and the two other flukes pre-dominantly in the plexus of veins surrounding the lower bowel. The male flukes are about 1 cm long and curve inwards to give a cylindrical appearance. They are paired with female flukes which are rather longer and more thread-like in appearance.

Eggs of *Schistosomiasis haematobium* laid into the blood vessels escape through the tissues into the bladder, and those of *Schistosomiasis mansoni* and *Schistosomiasis japonicum* escape into the rectum. The passage of eggs is traumatic and the former parasite causes urinary symptoms, in particular blood is passed in the urine and the latter two parasites cause profound diarrhoea.

Eggs escape in the urine or faeces and hatch in fresh water to produce a free-swimming larval form which is infective only to certain fresh-water snails. After penetration of the soft tissues of the snail, considerable multiplication of the parasite occurs and eventually the final larval forms, called cercaria, are produced. These break out of the snail and swim actively in water. On gaining contact with a human host they are able to penetrate skin and pass through tissues until they reach veins. After migrating through the heart and lungs they reach the particular veins in which development to the adult form takes place.

It will have been noted that parasitic infections are very numer-ous and widely distributed throughout the world. Many immi-grants arriving in this country are, therefore, likely to harbour parasites and their health may be affected by them. The majority are unaware of the presence of helminths but even when no definite symptoms are produced it is reasonable to assume that they are harmful. In the absence of reinfection, many parasites will gradually be eliminated but this may take several years and in the majority of cases detection and treatment are clearly desirable.

This brief description of some of the parasites and their various modes of transmission will have been sufficient to indicate that the chances of spread in this country are very slight. Water carriage disposal of faeces minimizes the risk of contamination of the soil with ova of soil transmitted helminths and prevents the spread of snail transmitted helminths. The absence of mosquitoes and blood-sucking flies from our cities eliminates the likelihood of arthropod-born infections and the food inspection service successfully limits the spread of helminths using the food-animal intermediate host. There remains the single possibility of the directly transmitted infections which, it is known, require close domestic contact with infested persons. The possibility of spread of infection within English schools has been investigated and no cross infection with helminthic parasites has been demonstrated. While there remains a slight theoretical risk it cannot be regarded as significant and in the circumstances prevailing here it is probable that the parasites will disappear within a relatively short time.

L

Action to be taken by the Health Department
following the arrival of an immigrant and his family

IT IS useful to have a routine procedure which is followed when information is received concerning the arrival of an immigrant, with or without his family. This system should be both extensive and flexible: it should cover most needs, but be capable of modification by omitting those parts which are unnecessary. The degree of community support afforded by the immigrants' own countrymen and women will be an important modifying factor: if information and advice can reach all newly arriving immigrants through their own community, so much the better. It will be vital for the Health Department, and other Local Government Departments, to have effective and continuous liaison with the local immigrant communities where these exist, and to encourage their establishment where they do not.

As soon as possible after the arrival of an immigrant and his family the household should be visited and the following arranged or advised as appropriate:

a) Information given with regard to the medical services and the advisability of being taken on the list of a local family doctor as soon as possible.

b) Arrangements made for Heaf testing and chest X-ray of all who have not had this done. BCG immunization to follow if indicated.

c) If children of school age have arrived, registration with the local education authority or with the Head of the local school, according to the arrangements obtaining in the area.

d) If children of under school age have arrived, a visit by the Health Visitor should be arranged so that she may introduce herself to the family and advise and arrange such immunization as may be necessary.

It is advisable that all children entering school have a medical examination as soon as possible. If arrangements can be made for this to be done before school entry but without causing any delay, this is generally preferable. It must be emphasized that the purpose of this examination is firstly, to discover if any defect requiring remedial treatment is present: secondly, to establish the presence of any disease requiring treatment and thirdly, to commence any immunizations which may be necessary.

The first visit is a most important one, especially if the immigrant family has little or no experience of life in this country. It may be that the newcomers' experience with authority to date, either in this country or their own, may not have been entirely happy: it is vital therefore that the first impression is for good rather than ill. Experience has shown that if a good relationship is established at the outset, future work is made much easier.

Immunization and Vaccination

THE diseases against which all children should be immunized are whooping cough, diphtheria, tetanus, poliomyelitis, measles, smallpox and tuberculosis. The first four of these immunizations are usually given in the first year of life, and measles and smallpox immunization are given in the second year of life. At school entry a booster immunization against diphtheria, tetanus and poliomyelitis is given to those who have had the primary course: otherwise a primary immunization course is started. School leavers should be given BCG if necessary and a booster immunization against poliomyelitis and tetanus.

Almost all immigrants arriving in this country will have been vaccinated against smallpox, and this therefore is unlikely to be required. If the child is over four years of age, immunization against whooping cough may be omitted from the primary course. The intervals between the three immunizations of the primary course are two months between the first and second, and four–six months between the second and third injections. In general there should be a minimum interval of one month between different immunizations. It is advisable that pregnant women be immunized against poliomyelitis, and three doses of oral vaccine should be given at intervals of one month: although no untoward effects have been reported, it is best to avoid routine immunization using the oral vaccine in the first three months of pregnancy. BCG immunization has already been dealt with.

Vaccination against smallpox in relation to other immunizing procedures

This often gives rise to a certain amount of difficulty. While each case must be taken on its individual merits, the following are the general principles involved. Basically it is unwise to give more than one immunizing agent at a time and there should ideally be a period of at least twenty-one days between each immunization. The reason is that the antigenic response of the body may be less than that desired if multiple antigens are given; the exception to this is triple immunization against whooping cough, tetanus and diphtheria (which is usually combined with oral poliomyelitis vaccine) when the various antigens are carefully balanced and a satisfactory antigenic response is obtained by their simultaneous use.

Immunization against smallpox using vaccinia virus is accompanied in a small number of cases by untoward complications. The frequency of complications is higher in the case of primary vaccination and it is therefore considered advisable to avoid immunization against certain other diseases at the same time. At least two weeks, and preferably three weeks should elapse between immunization against whooping cough, diphtheria, tetanus or cholera and primary smallpox vaccination, and three weeks between the administration of oral polio vaccine or measles vaccine and smallpox primary vaccination. Tuberculin testing and BCG vaccination should not be carried out within three weeks of primary vaccination against smallpox and the arm used for BCG vaccination should not be used for other immunizing procedures for six months.

In the case of vaccination against yellow fever and smallpox, yellow fever immunization is best given first and, if this is done, primary vaccination against smallpox can be given after four days; if primary vaccination against smallpox is done first, then there should be an interval of at least twenty-one days before yellow fever vaccine is given. In the case of a revaccination against smallpox, this can be done at the same time as vaccination against yellow fever, but it is best to give yellow fever vaccine first and to wait four days before revaccinating against smallpox.

Often there is insufficient time to allow for the optimum intervals between all immunizations and in this case a balance must be struck between protection of the individual and the avoidance of complications. The intervals between vaccination against smallpox and immunization against yellow fever should be regarded as mandatory and only to be broken in case of exposure to a known case of smallpox: other intervals may have to be reduced but the use of two live viruses together should be avoided—the risk is probably very small in the case of oral poliomyelitis immunization; measles immunization and primary smallpox vaccination should have at least two weeks between them if the measles vaccine is given first, and three weeks if smallpox vaccination is done first.

If vaccination against smallpox has to be done in the presence of a contra-indication, taking into acount the risks involved, then anti-vaccinal hyperimmune gammaglobulin is administered at the same time as the vaccination is done. It should be noted that gammaglobulin should not be given intravenously.

On general grounds it is best to avoid immunization using a live virus in the first trimester of pregnancy: however, there have been no specific instances of complications and, if vaccination and immunization procedures are considered advisable, then they should be done regardless of the stage of pregnancy.

Vital Statistics

THE TYPE of vital statistics referred to in this brief section are those beloved of the demographer and not those of more general interest to the judges involved in the selection of Miss *** of 1981.

Many matters concerning the birth, life and death of each individual in this and other countries are recorded. From them various conclusions are drawn and these are often expressed in the form of rates which indicate the average extent of the particular happening in question per unit amount of the population. Usually the rate is so many deaths, births, etc. per 1,000 of the general population. Two or more rates may be compared by a direct comparison quoting the particular rates or by an indirect one which gives a ratio expressing the difference between the rates—e.g. twice as much, a quarter as often, etc. It must be remembered that ratios do not indicate the frequency of the happening, merely the relative frequency of similar happenings in two different population groups. It must also be remembered that ratios or direct comparison are never meaningful unless the two happenings are comparable and unless the populations in whom a characteristic is being described are comparable.

For example, Brand X may wash twice as well, but if it washes twice as well as a piece of cheese, it is not likely to be much benefit to the Monday wash.

In order to prepare any vital statistics, the details of the population in which the happenings summarized in these statistics are occuring, must be accurately known. The number and the age and sex distribution of the population must be known, or no statistics can be prepared at all. If some are, then they are utterly invalid and misleading. The reason why so much attention is given by the Registrar General to the production of an accurate census is an index of the necessity of such information in the preparation of vital statistics.

Public Health is a non-static concept and is ever changing. The study of the public health is an applied science in that establishment of knowledge is done in order to apply that knowledge to the subject. The collection of vital statistics as an applied science is only justifiable in terms of the betterment of the public health: it is the aim of an effective health department continually to modify its work in the field of public health by the continuing assessment of the state of the public health by the collection of accurate and relevant data. The matter is therefore never static and data tends to be out-of-date soon after it is collected: this is a desirable state of affairs as the aim is continually to improve as well as prevent from becoming worse: this implies a constantly changing system.

The last main census in this country was taken in 1961 and a large proportion of some immigrant groups have entered this country since that date. It is therefore difficult to estimate the immigrant population with much accuracy, and impossible to establish the age and sex distribution. This means that although a crude rate (for example, of births) may be given within reasonably wide limits of accuracy, it is impossible to establish comparative rates as these depend on the age and sex structure of the populations concerned. An example may make this clearer.

Let us take two towns, each of comparable size and situation; in them reproduction is confined to the age group 20–45 and is at the same rate in each town. Let us call these towns A & B. The only difference between the two towns is the age distribution: the sex distribution is the same. In town A, the age distribution is 0–20 years, 30 per cent; 20–45 years, 40 per cent; and 45–100 years or more, 30 per cent. In town B the distribution is 0–20 years, 20 per cent; 20–45 years, 60 per cent; and 45–100 years or more, 20 per cent. Assuming the reproduction rate of the 20–45 years group to be 50 per 1,000 persons in that group, then the crude birth rate of town A will be 20 per 1,000 and that of town B 30 per 1,000: a difference which might give rise to many false conclusions if the incomparability of the crude rates was not realized. The example is illustrated in figure 7 (page 170).

Fig. 7

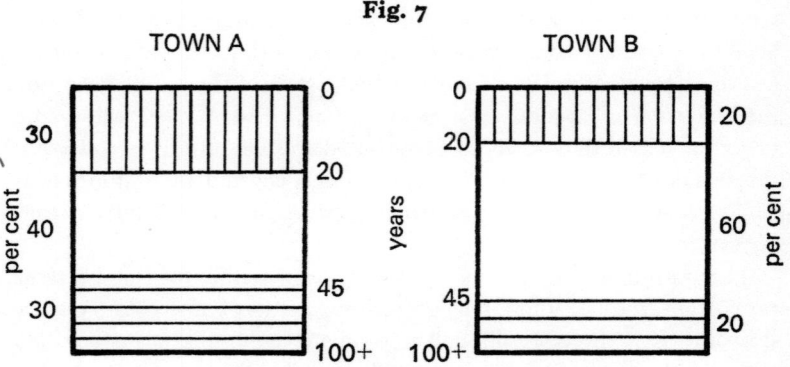

If the reproduction rate of the total population (male and female) age 20 − 45 years is 50 per 1,000: then the crude birth rate for 'A'

$$= \frac{50 \times 1,000 \times 40}{100}$$

$$= 20 \text{ per } 1,000$$

while for 'B' it is

$$\frac{50 \times 1,000 \times 60}{100}$$

Housing Standards of Fitness

STANDARD OF FITNESS state that a house must, after repair:

(1) be in a good state of repair and substantially free from damp:

(2) have each room properly lighted and ventilated:

(3) have adequate supply of wholesome water laid on inside the dwelling:

(4) be provided with efficient and adequate means of supplying hot water for domestic purposes:

(5) have an internal, otherwise readily accessible water closet:

(6) have a fixed bath or shower, preferably in a separate room:

(7) be provided with a sink or sinks and with suitable arrangements for disposal of hot water:

(8) have a proper drainage system:

(9) be provided in each room with adequate points for gass or electric lighting (where reasonably available):

(10) be provided with adequate facilities for heating:

(11) have satisfactory facilities for storage, preparation and cooking of food:

(12) have proper provision for the storage of fuel (when required).

(Reference: *Standards of Fitness, 1954*).

NOTE: These standards are an aim to be achieved rather than a legal standard to be enforced: they are the mark of a 'satisfactory' house, rather than a 'fit' one.

Housing Act, 1957—Part 2

A house is deemed 'unfit for human habitation' if, and *only* if, it is so far defective under one or more of the following headings, that it is not suitable for occupation:

(1) repair;

(2) stability;

(3) freedom from damp;

(4) natural lighting;

(5) ventilation;

(6) water supply;

(7) drainage and sanitary conveniences;

(8) facilities for the storage and preparation and cooking of food and for the disposal of waste water.

Unfit Houses

A house which is 'unfit' can be dealt with in the following ways:

(1) *Repair*—if the unfitness is due to matters that can be remedied at reasonable cost, a Notice can be served on the owner requiring him to correct any defects in a stated period; if the owner fails to do the repairs, the Local Authority may undertake them and charge the owner accordingly.

(2) *Demolition*—if the house is so unfit as to be beyond repair at reasonable cost *and* no person is prepared to repair it to the satisfaction of the Local Authority, a Demolition Order is made. The house is vacated in a stated time and demolished within six weeks of the date on which it becomes empty. The Local Authority must serve a Notice on the owner and all other interested persons (for example, a mortgagee) before commencing demolition.

Closing Order

If a house or part of a house, including an underground room, is considered 'unfit for human habitation', a Local Authority can make a Closing Order on the house, room or rooms considered unfit.

Unfitness Orders

Local Authorities may submit to the Ministry of Housing and Local Government a list of houses for inclusion in an unfitness order which are unfit for human habitation and which are unsuitable for renovation at reasonable expense. (Town and Country Planning Act, 1947). The Minister may, in the absence of objections or after an Inquiry, confirm an Unfitness Order if he thinks fit. If an Order is confirmed, compensation is paid as if the land concerned had been compulsorily purchased under Part 3 of the Housing Act, 1957 as land included in a clearance area.

Clearance Areas

This is the commonest method by which slum property is eradicated.

The clearance area must consist of two or more dwellings: it must be self-contained and have a continuous boundary and the buildings in it need not all be houses, although there must be a minimum of five dwellings. Houses may be included in a clearance area if they are unfit for human habitation, badly arranged, or dangerous and injurious to the health of the inhabitants. A Local Authority must be capable of providing alternative accommodation for all persons displaced by clearance. A copy of the Local Authority's resolution, stating the number of persons residing in the area on a stated day must be forwarded to the Ministry of Housing and Local Government who must hold a local Inquiry for all interested persons if one or more objections are received.

Following the establishment of a Clearance Area, either a Clearance Order or a Compulsory Purchase Order must be made. Under a Clearance Order, the owner is responsible for demolition, although he may elect or be obliged to meet the costs of the Local Authority demolishing in the owner's default. Under a Compulsory Purchase Order, the Local Authority buys the site and demolishes it.

Rent Act, 1965

A Rent Officer established under the 1965 Rent Act is an adviser to both tenants and landlord. If his advice is rejected by either party, or by both, the matter may be referred to the Rent Tribunal as established by the Act.

Housing Grant

Under the present Housing Acts, a grant may be paid by the local Authority to the owner of a dwelling house for the provision of a hot water supply, bath, wash-hand basin, sink and water closet. This grant is 50 per cent of the total cost, up to a maximum grant of £155. The water closet would be inside the dwelling, or immediately accessible to it.

A new Housing Act is expected in 1969 which may alter the grant payable.

APPENDIX V

1967, Migrant Workers in Western Europe

(Figures from the Second Consultation of the Churches Committee on migrant workers in Western Europe—published Geneva, 1968)

Origin	Austria	France	Germany	Switzerland	Belgium	Holland	Sweden	U.K.	Total
Europe									
Greek	380 Ø	10,000	140,000	8,000	B 1,710	2,050	5,920	D* 4,000	177,060
Italian	1,430	700,000	266,800	510,000	B 68,160	7,500	5,420	D* 24,000	1,583,310
Maltese	—	—	—	—	—	—	—	D* 30,000	30,000
Portuguese	—	300,000	17,800	—	B 2,110	2,350	—	D* 4,000	326,260
Spanish	350	649,120	118,030	81,000	B 25,680	13,700	3,190	D* 25,000	907,070
Yugoslavian	45,480	40,000	97,720	11,000	B 8,000	1,450	13,420	D* 2,000	219,070
Middle East									
Cypriot	—	—	—	—	—	—	—	* 60,000	60,000
Turkish	6,500	5,500	131,300	7,000	7,270	10,700	—	1,500	169,000
Far East									
Chinese	—	2,610	540	—	—	—	—	AD* 3,000	6,150
Hong Kong	—	—	—	—	—	—	—	17,000	17,000
Indian	—	990	3,070	—	—	—	—	230,000	234,060
Korean	—	400	3,950	—	—	—	—	—	4,350
Malaysian	—	—	—	—	—	—	—	16,000	16,000

		(*1966)	(Ø1965)						Total
Pakistani	—	—	—	—	—	180	420	125,000	125,600
Singapore	—	—	—	—	—	—	—	18,000	18,000
America									
West Indies	—	—	—	—	—	—	—	445,000	445,000
Africa									
Algeria	—	600,000	1,480	B 1,710	—	—	—	—	603,190
Congolese	—	—	80	—	—	—	—	—	80
Ethiopian	—	200	70	—	—	—	—	—	270
Ghanain	—	—	280	—	—	—	—	—	280
Moroccan	—	100,000	5,820	B 13,370	12,520	—	—	—	131,710
Nigerian	—	—	610	—	—	—	—	—	610
South African	—	—	350	—	—	—	—	—	350
Sudanese	—	70	100	—	—	—	—	—	170
Togolese	—	—	220	—	—	—	—	—	220
Tunisian	—	60,000	Ø 760	B 430	700	—	—	—	61,890
i/C								93,000	93,000
i/A								79,000	79,000
Others	5,860	539,930	201,530	273,300	48,430	19,730	144,020	1,176,500	1,232,800
Total	60,000	3,000,000	991,250	891,000	181,560	70,000	171,970	6,542,280	6,542,280

A—non-commonwealth.
C—Commonwealth.
i—All African countries.
* 1966
Ø 1965
B—only migrants subject to registration with the Belgian Social Security.
D—registered with the police: after four years' residence aliens are normally exempt from further registration.

Others—includes groups and nationalities not necessarily migrant workers.

GLOSSARY

anorexia (noun)	literally, 'without appetite'.
anorexic (adjective)	*see above.*
anthelmintic drugs	drugs given to treat infection by helminths.
antigen	a substance capable of stimulating the body's immunological mechanism against itself.
antigenic strain	an antigen, specific to a particular strain or sub-strain of infecting organism.
arthropod	member of the largest phylum (group) in the animal kingdom; in which the exoskeleton is hard and jointed and the legs are paired and jointed as are the other appendages. Includes insects, spiders, centipedes etc.
autism (noun)	state of introversion in which the patient withdraws from reality into a phantasy world.
autistic (adjective)	*see above.*
BCG	Calmette-Guérin bacillus. A modified mammalian tuberculosis bacillus capable, when given by vaccination, of inducing resistance in the human body against natural tuberculosis.
chemotherapy	treatment of disease by chemical (pharmacological) substances.
communicable disease	a disease capable of being transmitted from one person to another.
contagious disease	an infectious disease capable of being transmitted by contact.
corrected rate	the 'crude rate' corrected and standardized for a standard population. The population structure (age/sex, etc.) of England and Wales is usually taken as the standard.
crude rate	the rate at which a happening occurs in a

population expressed as the number of happenings per unit size of population, regardless of population structure.

definitive host | the host of a parasite, in which sexual reproduction of the parasite occurs.

endemic (adjective) | a condition, generally an infectious disease, habitually present in a community.

endemicity | the degree to which a disease common to an area is generally present.

epidemic | an outbreak of infectious disease affecting many people at the same time; the outbreak usually reaches a peak and then subsides.

epidemiology | the study of the natural history of disease in the community: often applied particularly to infectious disease but can be used to refer to the study of the natural history of all phenomena as they affect the community—as opposed to the effect on the individual.

epileptiform (convulsions) | spasmodic convulsions resembling those due to epilepsy.

gastro-enteritis | an infective inflammation of the stomach and intestine, giving rise to vomiting and diarrhoea.

haemoglobin | the red pigment of mammalian blood present in the red blood cell and responsible for carrying oxygen. A deficiency of haemoglobin is known as anaemia.

helminths | worms. Usually applied to parasitic worms.

immigrant | a person travelling to a country which is not his own and taking up residence for a minimum of one year.

immunization | the process of inducing the production of immune substances by the body or the artificial injection of these substances.

immunological state | the state of the protective mechanisms of the body effective against specific diseases.

immunology | the study of the protective mechanism

M

present in the body and active against disease.

incubation period — the period between the initial infection and the development of the symptoms of the disease.

indigenous community — that part of the community already established in an area.

infectious — a disease or condition capable of being transmitted from one person to another.

infectious disease — a disease due to the growth of micro-organisms in the body and capable of being transmitted from one person to another.

intermediate host — the host of a parasite in which sexual reproduction of the parasite does not occur.

morbidity rate — the number of these suffering from a specific disease.

mortality (rate) — death (rate) resulting from a specific disease.

mycobacteria — bacteria of the type responsible for tuberculous infection. A number of different strains exist; generally these are specific for a particular host.

neurosis — a mental disorder, often presenting as a bodily symptom without demonstrable physical lesion. Awareness of reality is not lost.

notifiable disease — a disease the presence of which must be notified to the local health authority.

papule — a 'spot' raised above the surface of the skin.

paranoia — a psychosis in which delusions of persecution may arise; the patient may be violent because of these delusions.

polygamy — a state in which a man can have more than one legal wife.

population — the total number of people living in a particular area, or a defined part of that total.

prophylactic drug — a drug given to prevent the emergence of a disease; usually applicable to a communicable disease.

psychosis — an abnormal mental state in which the patient's appreciation of his world is distorted and he loses contact with reality.

psycho-somatic — the modification of physical symptoms by the underlying mental state; the latter often being more important.

purdah — the curtain dividing the house and screening the women from the visitor's sight. Often used in the sense of screening women from the sight of men other than the husband.

quarantinable disease — a serious infectious disease in which, to prevent the spread of infection, the patient suffering from the disease may be isolated until he is no longer able to infect others.

reservoir (of infection) — the disease present in a community from which further infection may occur in circumstances favourable to that disease.

surveillance — the process by which a person who may be in the incubation stage of a disease is visited regularly so that, if he develops the disease, necessary action may be taken.

vaccination — the practice of inducing the production of immune substances by the body by the injection of a vaccine.

vaccine — a substance capable of inducing immunity via the normal body mechanisms when artificially introduced into the body.

BOOK LIST

—ARCHER (Ed.), *Social Welfare and the Citizen,* Penguin Books, Harmondsworth.

BROCKINTON FRASER, *World Health,* Penguin Books, Harmondsworth.

CIBA FOUNDATION, *Immigration—Medical and Social Aspects,* Churchill.

—CLEGG and —MEGSON, *Children in Distress,* Penguin Books, Harmondsworth.

ELLIS, R. W. B., *Health in Childhood,* Penguin Books, Harmondsworth.

GALE, A. H., *Epidemic Diseases,* Penguin Books, Harmondsworth.

GILES, F. T., *Children and the Law,* Penguin Books, Harmonsdworth.

HUXLEY, ELSPETH, *Back Street, New Worlds,* Chatto & Windus, Ltd. 1964.

LAPAGE, GEOFFREY, *Animals parasitic in Man,* Dover: Constable and Penguin Books, Harmondsworth.

MINISTRY OF HEALTH: Pamphlet No. 43, *English for Immigrants,* H.M.S.O.

—NICHOLSON, *Mother and Baby Homes,* Allen and Unwin Ltd.

V.D.—The Facts, A *Family Doctor* booklet, British Medical Association.

—WIMPERIS, *The Unmarried Mother and her Child,* Allen and Unwin Ltd.

Various leaflets on venereal disease is published by the Central Council for Health Education, Tavistock Square, London WC1.

The National Committee for Commonwealth Immigrants, 6 Tilney Street, London W1, issue a number of publications; these are very reasonably priced and contain much useful information. The following publications are obtainable.

The Housing of Commonwealth Immigrants.

Areas of Special Housing Need.

Practical Suggestions for Teachers of Immigrant Children.

Research and the Teaching of Immigrant Children: R. Goldman.

The Education of West Indian Immigrant Children: P. C. C. Evans.

The Indian Family in Britain: Dilip Hiro.

Racial Discrimination.

Anti-Discrimination Regulation.

Public Health Aspects of Immigration: J. F. Skone.
Race in the Curriculum.
Towards a Multi-Racial Society.
The Young Englanders: Stuart Hall.
The Pakistani Family in Britain: Farrulch Hashmi.
Prejudice in the Community: David Stafford-Clark.
Health and Welfare of the Immigrant Child: Simon Yudkin.
Psychology of Racial Prejudice: Farrukh Hashmi.

Information on facilities for the care of the unmarried mother and her child may be obtained from the National Council for the Unmarried Mother and her Child, 255 Kentish Town Road, London NW5. Many local authorities also have information on this matter. The Council will also be able to supply statistical and other information.

The Family Planning Association, Margaret Pyke House, 27–35 Mortimer Street, London W1, will be able to recommend and supply books on family planning and sex education.

INDEX

adaptation, stress of, 103
adolescence, 35
age of children, 39
aliens, 45
anaemia, 89
ante-natal clinics, 77
ante-natal examination, 77
ante-natal health education, 81
ascaris, 155
Asian girls, selection of suitors, 35

B.C.G. vaccination, 130
bilharzia, 159
birthrate, crude, effect on population distribution, 168–70
bodies, removal from England, 44

care of children by local authority, 94
change of home, mental stresses, 71
childcare by relatives, 103
child-minding, 96, 106
children, non-English-speaking, 100
cholera, 127
clearance areas, 172
climate, 39
closing order, 172
clothing, 39
Commonwealth Immigration Act, 1962, 46
Commonwealth Immigration Act, 1968, 52
communication barriers, 15
communication, midwife to patient, 80
contact tracing, tuberculosis, 139
contact tracing, V.D., 148
control of tuberculosis in immigrant population, 131
control, V.D., 145

corrected rates, 168–70
cremation, 43–44
crude rates, 168–70
custom, differences in dress, 101

dead, disposal of, 43
demolition, 172
diet, 30
diet, religious prohibition of foods, 29
diphtheria, 126
discipline at home and at school, 104
discrimination, unlawful, 54
divorce, 33
dress, 101

environmental influences, 24
eradication of tuberculosis, 131

family planning, 86
family disruption, 72, 75
families, division of, 97
fasts, 30
fasts, Ramadan, 30, 80
feeding, infant, 81
fevers of unknown origin, 123
filariasis, 158
fire hazards, 40
fire, risk of, 61
'Folk Devil' myth, 15
Food and Drugs Act, 67
food hygiene regulations, 65
food poisoning, 109
food premises, 65
food shops, 65
foster parents, 95

gastro-enteritis, 82
gonorrhea, incidence of, 142

Heaf test, 133
health department, action by on arrival of immigrant, 163
health education, ante-natal, 81
heating, 40
helminthic infection, 153
hereditary diseases, 22
Hinduism, 28
hookworm, 156
Housing Act, 1957, 59
Housing Act 1957, part 2, 171
housing associations, 61
houses, demolition of, 172
housing grant, 173
house purchase, 62
house repair, 172
housing shortages, 57
housing, standards of fitness, 171
housing trusts, 62
housing, unfit, 172
hygiene, general, 41

illegitimacy, 36
immigrants returning to their own country, 24
immigration, causes of, 13
immigration, details of numbers, 46–49, 174–5
immigration, 1965 White Paper, 50
immunization, cholera, 123
immunization of immigrant child, 165
immunization of immigrant on arrival, 163
immunization of pregnant women against poliomyelitis, 165
immunization, poliomyelitis, 125
immunization, smallpox, 115
immunization, yellow fever, 115
imported disease, 122
infectious disease regulations, 107
infective enteritis, 82
influence of population movement on disease, 20–22
international certificates of immunization, 113

international sanitary regulations, 110
Islam, 28
isolation, 113

leprosy, 127

malaria, 128
marriage and divorce, 33
mass miniature radiography, 132
mass X-ray, 132
meat, regulations concerning handling, 68
mental illness in adults, 72
mental illness in children, 75
multiple occupation of houses, 58

names and naming, 36
notifiable disease, 107
nutrition disease, 90–92

onchocerciasis, 159
over-crowding, 58

paraffin heaters, 40
paratyphoid, 124
play, restriction of, 97
poliomyelitis, 124
poliomyelitis immunization, 125
polygamy, 34
population, growth due to immigration, 13
population movement, 17
population movement, types of, 17
population structure, changes in, 25
prejudice, racial, 14
purdah, 32

quarantinable disease, 110, 113

Race Relations Act, 1968, 54
Ramadan, 30
religion, 28
religious prohibition of foods, 29
Rent Act, 1965, 173
rental purchase, 63
rented houses, 61

repairs, responsibility for, 63
rickets, 85, 91
roundworm, 155

salvars, 101
sanitation, 41
schistosomiasis, 159
school meals, 92, 102
school medical examination, 99
school/parent contact, 102
scurvy, 92
Shops Act (The), 69
Sikhism, 29
slaughterhouses, 68
slum clearance, 64
smallpox vaccination, 165
social services, deficiencies in, 13, 14
statistics relating to immigration, 174-5
statistics, vital, 168
Street Offences Act, 145
stress (adaptation), 103
stress following change of home, 71
strongyloides, 157
sub-nutrition, 89
surveillance, 113, 117
syphilis incidence, 142

taenia, 153
tapeworm, 153
tapeworm, dwarf, 154
threadworm, 153
trachoma, 126
trichuris, 156
tuberculin test, 133
tuberculosis, 130
tuberculosis, control of (general), 130
tuberculosis control in immigrant populations, 131

tuberculosis, eradication of, 131
typhoid, 124

unfit housing, 171, 172
unfitness order (housing), 172
under-nutrition of children, 31

vaccination, B.C.G., 134
vaccination of immigrant child, 165
vaccination, smallpox, 165
vaccination, timing, 165
vaccination, yellow fever, 166
vegetarian nutrition, 92
vegetarian food, weaning, 83
venereal disease, 142
venereal disease and the law, 143
venereal disease, ante-natal examination, 146
venereal disease, causes of, 142
venereal disease, confidentiality of documents, 145
venereal disease, contact tracing, 148
venereal disease, control, 145
venereal disease, incidence, 142
venereal disease, pre-marital examination, 146
vital statistics, 168
voucher-holders, 47
vouchers, 47

weaning, 81
weaning, religious prohibition of foods, 83
weaning, vegetarian foods, 83
whipworm, 156
worms, 153

X-ray, mass, 132

yaws, 125

THE FIELD WORKER IN
IMMIGRANT HEALTH

28 July